CHILDREN'S ATLAS

Philip Steele

DP
DEMPSEY
PARR

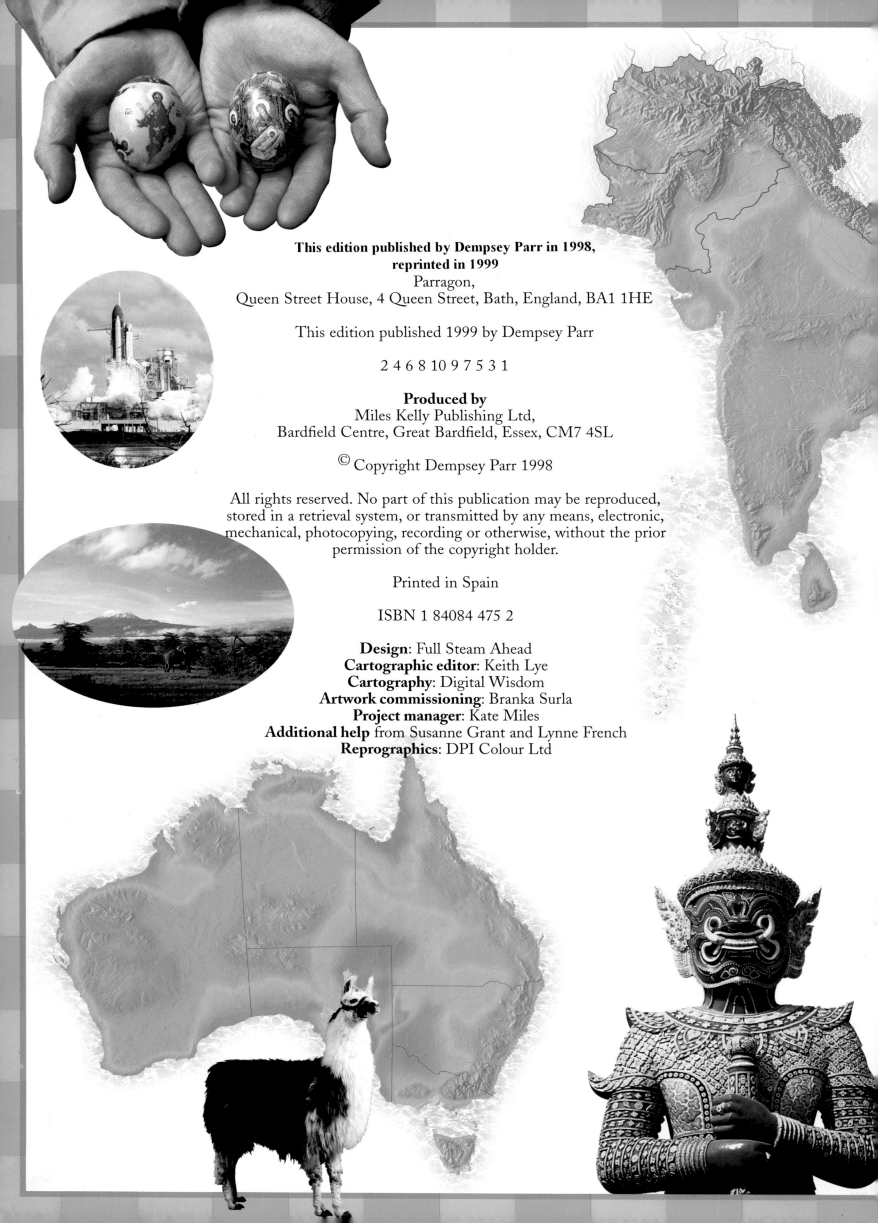

**This edition published by Dempsey Parr in 1998,
reprinted in 1999**
Parragon,
Queen Street House, 4 Queen Street, Bath, England, BA1 1HE

This edition published 1999 by Dempsey Parr

2 4 6 8 10 9 7 5 3 1

Produced by
Miles Kelly Publishing Ltd,
Bardfield Centre, Great Bardfield, Essex, CM7 4SL

Printed in Spain

ISBN 1 84084 475 2

Design: Full Steam Ahead
Cartographic editor: Keith Lye
Cartography: Digital Wisdom
Artwork commissioning: Branka Surla
Project manager: Kate Miles
Additional help from Susanne Grant and Lynne French
Reprographics: DPI Colour Ltd

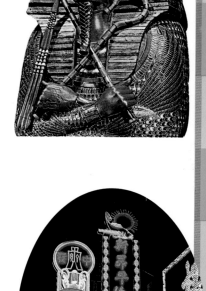

CONTENTS

CONTENTS

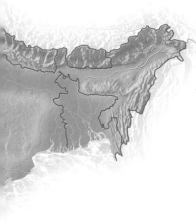

How to use this Atlas	4
Earth Facts	5
Countries of the World	6-7
Scandinavia and Finland	8-9
Low Countries	10-11
British Isles	12-13
France and Monaco	14-15
Germany and the Alps	16-17
Iberian Peninsula	18-19
Italy and its Neighbors	20-21
Central Europe	22-23
Balkans and Romania	24-25
Russia and its Neighbors	26-27
Canada and Greenland	28-29
USA	30-33
Mexico, Central America, and the Caribbean	34-35
North Andean Countries	36-37
Brazil and its Neighbors	38-39
Argentina and its Neighbors	40-41
Southwest Asia	42-43
India and its Neighbors	44-45
China and its Neighbors	46-47
Japan	48-49
Southeast Asia	50-51
North and West Africa	52-53
Central, Eastern, and Southern Africa	54-55
Australia	56-57
New Zealand and the Pacific	58-59
Polar Lands	60
Index	61-64

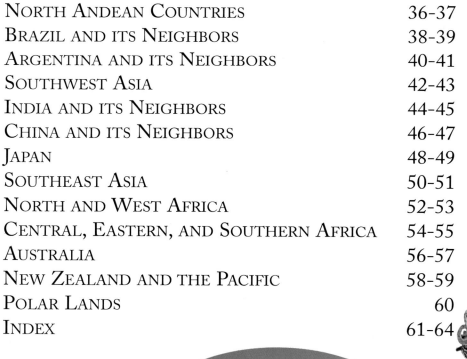

HOW TO USE THIS ATLAS

WELCOME TO THE PLANET EARTH! This atlas shows you the world we live in. An atlas is any large book of maps. Maps are plans that show the surface of a planet as if it was flat, instead of round. They show the lie of the land, the rivers and coastlines, mountains and seas.

Maps that just show the details of the landscape are called "physical." Maps that just show the borders of countries, states, counties or provinces are called "political." The maps in this book show the physical details of the land, but they show national borders and major cities as well. Maps use signs and symbols to give you more information. Look at the key to find out what they mean.

So how do you find the city or country you are looking for? First of all look up the name you want in the index on p.61. When you have found the right page, look for the name on the big map of the region. Next to each regional map, look for the little map which helps you to see at a glance which part of the world is being shown.

Next, read the words to find out more about the countries, the climate of the region, the peoples and how they live. Small boxes also give you key facts and figures about each of the countries. They tell you the area, the population size, the name of the capital city, the country's official language or languages, and the currency, or type of money, used by the people there.

When you read about distant lands, it may help to compare them with where you live. Are they bigger or smaller, hotter or wetter, more crowded? You might use the maps to do a bit of detective work. Can you work out why most Australian cities are near the coast, or why most Canadian cities are in the south of the country?

Colors
On this map, the different colors show you at a glance the physical features of the landscape. Each color represents a type of geographic feature.

Spot the mountain
This symbol means "mountain." The mountain's name is printed next to it, along with the height of the summit above sea level. The height is given in feet.

N for north
This symbol represents a compass, with its magnetic needle pointing due north.

Capital cities
The most important town in any country is called the capital city. This is very often the biggest town and is normally where the government makes the laws. Some capitals, however, are quite small.

Coastlines and borders
The borders of Japan are natural, because the country is made up of islands. Other countries may have land borders, marked by a line on the map.

Where in the world
If you want to find out where the regional map fits into a map of the whole world, check these small circular maps. The areas colored in red show the location.

Key to symbols

■	Capitals
●	Towns
—	Rivers
—	Borders
🗺	Lakes
▦	Mountains

4

INTRODUCTION

EARTH FACTS

The world we live in is a huge ball of rock and metal spinning around, or rotating, in space. As the planet Earth rotates, it travels around the Sun, held on its path by a pulling force called gravity. The Earth is one of nine planets circling the Sun, and together they make up the Solar System.

When we see pictures of Earth taken from space, our planet appears blue, white, and brown. The blue is the color of the seas and oceans that cover more than two thirds of the Earth's surface. The swirling white patterns are the clouds—water vapor which hangs in the air, or atmosphere, surrounding the Earth's surface. The brown is the color of the ground, which is divided into the Earth's land masses or continents.

Photographs of the Earth's surface taken from space zoom in to show even more details—the world's great river systems, the high mountain ranges, the sprawling cities, and the patchwork of crops that feed the hungry mouths of the world's population, which is expected to reach more than 6.1 billion by the year 2000.

PLANET EARTH
Circumference around the Equator: 24,846 miles
Circumference around the Poles: 24,805 miles
Diameter at the Equator: 7,909 miles
Surface area: About 196,000,000 square miles
Area covered by sea: 71 percent
Average distance from the Sun: 92,752,000 miles
Average distance from the Moon: 238,700 miles
Period of rotation: 23 hours 56 minutes
Speed of rotation: 1,029 miles per hour at the Equator
Period of revolution: 365 days 6 hours
Speed of revolution: 18.5 miles per second

FACT BOX

The world's highest peak
Mount Everest or Qomolangma, between Nepal and China, is the highest point on the Earth's surface.

HIGHEST PEAKS

Mountain	Height	Location
Everest (Qomolangma)	29,021 ft	China-Nepal
K2 (Qogir Feng)	28,244 ft	India-Pakistan
Kanchenjunga	28,162 ft	India-Nepal
Makalu 1	27,759 ft	China-Nepal
Dhaulagiri 1	26,788 ft	Nepal
Nanga Parbat	26,650 ft	India
Annapurna 1	26.538 ft	Nepal
Gosainthan (Xixabangma Feng)	826,279 ft	China
Distaghil Sar	25,863 ft	India
Nanda Devi	25,636 ft	India

LONGEST RIVERS

River	Length	Location
Nile	4,135 miles	North Africa
Amazon	3,998 miles	South America
Chang Jiang (Yangtze)	3,906 miles	Central China
Mississippi-Missouri-Red	3,732 miles	North America
Yenisey-Angara-Selenga	3,435 miles	Mongolia-Russia
Huang He	3,388 miles	Northern China
Ob-Irtysh	3,354 miles	Russia-Kazakhstan
Zaïre (Congo)	2,914 miles	Central Africa
Lena-Kirenga	2,728 miles	Russia
Mekong	2,697 miles	Southeast Asia

LARGEST LAKES

Lake	Area	Location
Caspian Sea	142,920 sq miles	Central Asia
Superior	31,560 sq miles	USA-Canada
Victoria	26,710 sq miles	East Africa
Aral Sea	25,178 sq miles	Central Asia
Huron	22,898 sq miles	USA-Canada
Michigan	22,202 sq miles	USA-Canada
Tanganyika	12,644 sq miles	East Africa
Baikal	12,809 sq miles	Russia
Great Bear	12,042 sq miles	Canada
Malawi	11,101 sq miles	Southern Africa

LARGEST ISLANDS

Island	Area
Greenland	839,145 sq miles
New Guinea	315,592 sq miles
Borneo	279,805 sq miles
Madagascar	226,443 sq miles
Baffin	195,742 sq miles
Sumatra	166,054 sq miles
Honshu	87,722 sq miles
Great Britain	84,107 sq miles
Victoria	81,570 sq miles
Ellesmere	75,695 sq miles

MAJOR WATERFALLS

Highest Waterfalls

	Height	Location
Angel Falls	3,211 ft	Venezuela
Mardsalsfossen	2,539 ft	Norway
Yosemite	2,424 ft	United States

Greatest volume

Waterfall	Volume	Location
Boyoma	600,000 cu ft per sec	Dem. Rep. Congo (Zaïre)

OCEANS

Name	Area
Pacific	63,903,400 sq miles
Atlantic	40,746,400 sq miles
Indian	28,253,400 sq miles
Arctic	5,516,400 sq miles

COUNTRIES OF THE WORLD

To the glory of God
Places of worship vary greatly around the world. This Christian cathedral, St. Basil's, was built in the 1500s in Moscow, capital of today's Russian Federation.

There are 192 countries in the world that are recognized as "independent" nations, which means that they govern themselves. Many other lands are colonies or "dependencies," which means that they are governed by other nations. The numbers change very often, as one country joins up with another one, or another splits up into separate nations. For example, Eritrea was part of Ethiopia until 1991, when it broke away to become an independent nation.

Some countries are huge, some are tiny. The Russian Federation is the largest, with an area of 6,564,793 square miles. The smallest is Vatican City, at just 0.15 square miles. Some countries are home to just one people, while others are made up of many different peoples or ethnic groups, each with their own way of life and customs. Some peoples have no national borders of their own. For example, the traditional homeland of the Kurdish people is divided between Turkey, Iraq, and Iran.

The peoples of the world live very different lives. They have different faiths and beliefs, eat different foods, and speak more than 5,000 different languages. Some people are very poor while others are very rich. However, the people on our planet also have many things in common. The spread of radio, television, and other communications links in recent years has made the world a smaller place. Once it took years to travel around the world, but today we can get on a plane or keep in touch with each other at the push of a button.

Most of the world's countries are linked by agreements or treaties. Many European countries belong to the European Union, while African nations belong to the Organization of African Unity. Nearly all countries belong to the United Nations, which tries to prevent conflict and to build links between the world's nations.

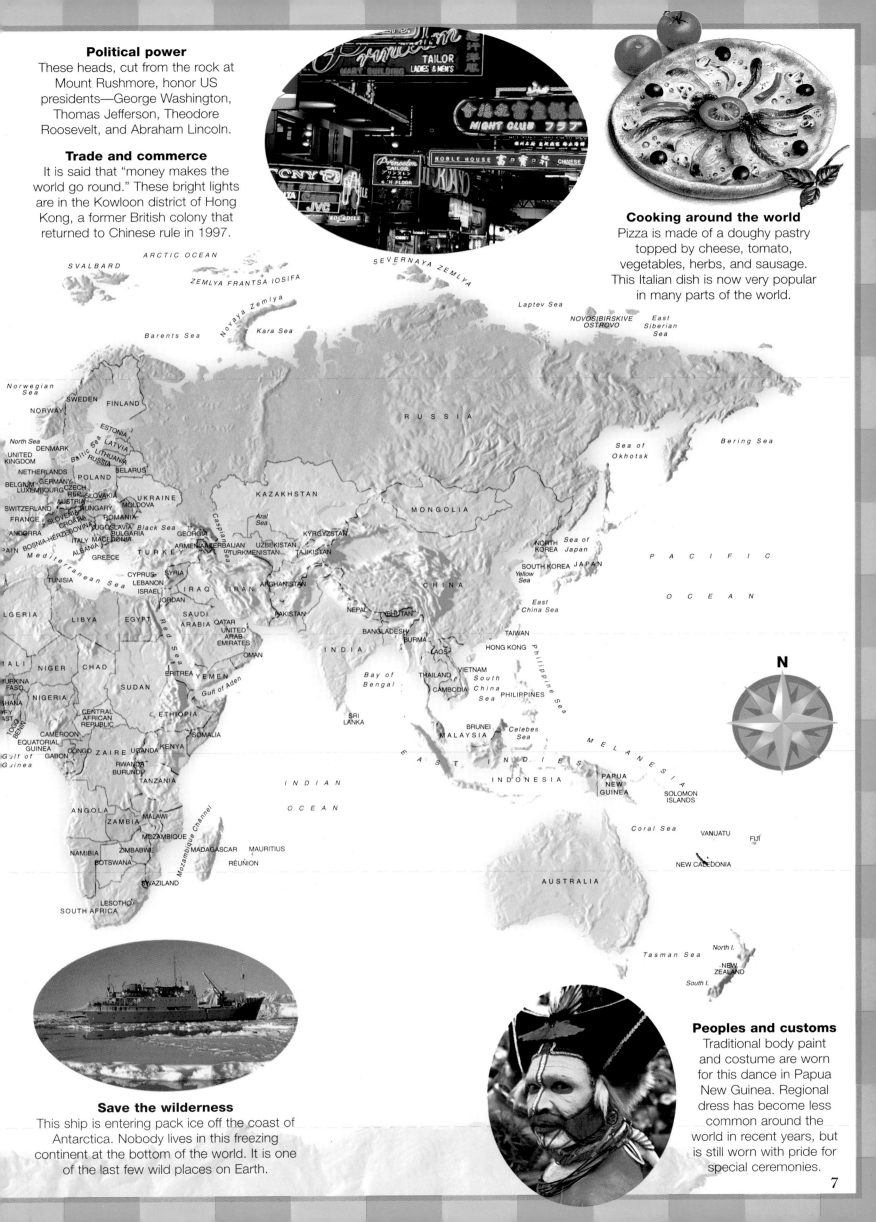

Political power
These heads, cut from the rock at Mount Rushmore, honor US presidents—George Washington, Thomas Jefferson, Theodore Roosevelt, and Abraham Lincoln.

Trade and commerce
It is said that "money makes the world go round." These bright lights are in the Kowloon district of Hong Kong, a former British colony that returned to Chinese rule in 1997.

Cooking around the world
Pizza is made of a doughy pastry topped by cheese, tomato, vegetables, herbs, and sausage. This Italian dish is now very popular in many parts of the world.

Save the wilderness
This ship is entering pack ice off the coast of Antarctica. Nobody lives in this freezing continent at the bottom of the world. It is one of the last few wild places on Earth.

Peoples and customs
Traditional body paint and costume are worn for this dance in Papua New Guinea. Regional dress has become less common around the world in recent years, but is still worn with pride for special ceremonies.

EUROPE

SCANDINAVIA AND FINLAND

FACT BOX

◆ Denmark
Area: 16,558 sq miles
Population: 5,300,000
Capital: Copenhagen
Official language: Danish
Currency: Danish krone

◆ Sweden
Area: 172,899 sq miles
Population: 8,000,000
Capital: Stockholm
Official language: Swedish
Currency: Krona

◆ Norway
Area: 124,505 sq miles
Population: 4,400,000
Capital: Oslo
Official language: Norwegian
Currency: Norwegian krone

◆ Finland
Area: 129 554 sq miles
Population: 5,100,000
Capital: Helsinki
Official language: Finnish
Currency: Markka

TWO PENINSULAS extend from northwestern Europe, shaped rather like the claws of a crab. The southern peninsula, extending from Germany, is called Jutland.

Together with a chain of islands which includes Fyn, Sjælland, and Lolland, Jutland makes up the nation of **Denmark**. Most of Denmark is flat and low-lying, a country of green farmland. It exports bacon and dairy products.

Across the windy channels of Sgagerrak and Kattegat, between the North and Baltic Seas, lies the long northern peninsula occupied by **Sweden** and **Norway**. This is a land shaped by movements of ice in prehistoric times. Glaciers carved out the deep sea inlets called fjords along its ragged western coast. Ranges of mountains run down the peninsula like a backbone. They descend to a land of forests, bogs, and thousands of lakes.

Summers can be warm, but winters are bitterly cold, with heavy snow. Norway lives by fishing and its North Sea rigs make it Western Europe's largest producer of oil and natural gas. Sweden is a major exporter of timber, paper, wooden furniture, and motor vehicles.

The three nations of Denmark, Sweden, and Norway form the region of Scandinavia. It was from here that the seafarers known as Vikings set out about 1,200 years ago. The Vikings raided and settled the coasts of Western Europe, traded in Russia and the Middle East, settled Iceland and Greenland and even reached North America. Today's Danes, Swedes and Norwegians are all closely related, as are the Germanic languages that they speak.

The Arctic lands of northern Scandinavia are home to the Saami (or Lapps), a people who traditionally lived by herding reindeer. Their neighbors are the Finns and the Russians.

Finland is a land of lakes, with coasts on the Gulfs of Bothnia and Finland. Its forests make it a leading producer of wood pulp and paper. Helsinki is the capital.

8

Map labels

RUSSIA

FINLAND

ICELAND

Hvannadalshnúkur 2,119m
VATNAJÖKULL
Neskaupstadur
Búdir
Djúpivogur
Höfn
Eskifjördur
Seydisfjördur
Vopnafjördur
Raufarhöfn
Kópasker
Jökulsá á Fjöllum
Húsavik
Myvatn
Olafsfjördur
Skálfandafljót
Akureyri
Saudárkrókur
HOFSJÖKULL
Grimsey
Blanda
Blönduós
Hvitá
HVÍTÁ
LANGJÖKULL
Þjórsá
Þórisvatn
Hekla 1,491 m
MYRDALSJÖKULL
Vík
Surtsey
Heimaey
Vestmannaeyjar
Stokkseyri
Þingvallavatn
Reykjavik
Keflavik
Akranes
Borgarnes
Stykkishólmur
Breidafjördur
Olafsvik
Hólmavik
Vatneyri
Thingeyri
Ísafjördur
Hunafloi

North Cape
Vadsø
Kirkenes
Polmak
Utsjoki
Inarijärvi
Karasjok
Alta
Hammerfest
Tromsø
Mt. Haltia 4,343 ft
Narvik
LOFOTEN VESTERÅLEN
Bodø
Mosjøen

LAPLAND
Enontekiö
Sodankylä
Pelkosenniemi
Rovaniemi
Kemi
Tornio
Oulu
Kajaani
Mt. Kebnekaise 6,924 ft
Kiruna
Vittangi
Gällivare
Jokkmokk
Sorsele
Storuman
Boden
Luleå
Piteå
Skellefteå
Skellefte å

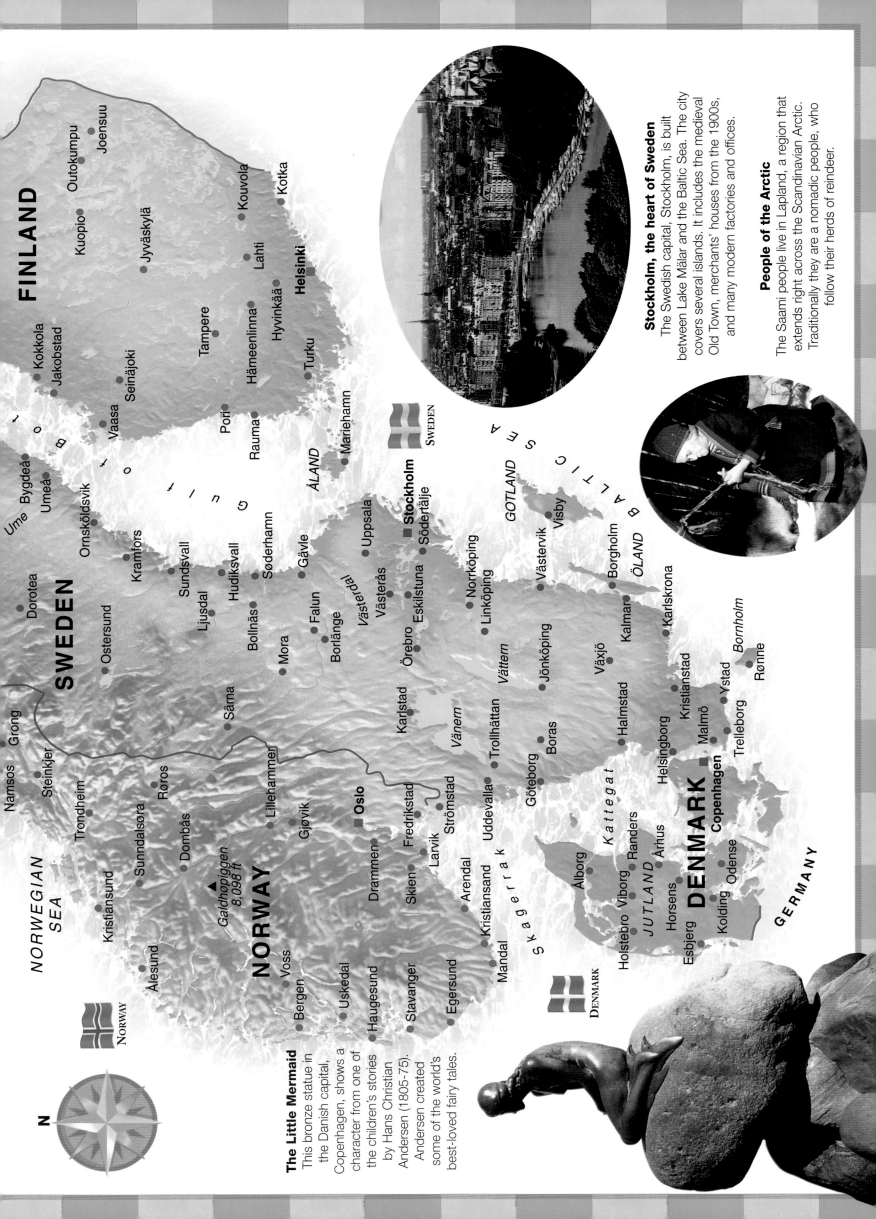

FINLAND

Joensuu
Outokumpu
Kuopio
Kokkola
Jakobstad
Jyväskylä
Seinäjoki
Tampere
Vaasa
Hämeenlinna
Lahti
Kouvola
Kotka
Hyvinkää
Helsinki
Pori
Rauma
Turku
Mariehamn
ÅLAND

Gulf of Bothnia

SWEDEN

Namsos
Grong
Steinkjer
Trondheim
Dorotea
Røros
Ostersund
Kramfors
Ornsköldsvik
Umeå
Bygdeå
Ume
Sundsvall
Hudiksvall
Söderhamn
Ljusdal
Bollnäs
Gävle
Sundsvall
Mora
Falun
Borlänge
Västerdal
Uppsala
Västerås
Stockholm
Södertälje
Eskilstuna
Örebro
Norrköping
Linköping
Visby
GOTLAND
Västervik
Särna
Karlstad
Vänern
Vättern
Jönköping
Borgholm
ÖLAND
Trollhättan
Boras
Växjö
Kalmar
Karlskrona
Göteborg
Halmstad
Kristianstad
Helsingborg
Malmö
Ystad
Bornholm
Trelleborg
Rønne

SWEDEN

BALTIC SEA

NORWAY

NORWEGIAN SEA
Ålesund
Kristiansund
Sunndalsøra
Voss
Bergen
Uskedal
Haugesund
Stavanger
Egersund
Mandal
Kristiansand
Arendal
Larvik
Skien
Fredrikstad
Strömstad
Uddevalla
Skagerrak
▲ *Galdhøpiggen*
8,098 ft
Dombås
Gjøvik
Lillehammer
Oslo
Drammen

NORWAY

DENMARK

Kattegat
Ålborg
Holstebro
Viborg
Randers
Århus
Horsens
JUTLAND
Esbjerg
Kolding
Odense
Copenhagen
Helsingborg

DENMARK

GERMANY

Stockholm, the heart of Sweden

The Swedish capital, Stockholm, is built between Lake Mälar and the Baltic Sea. The city covers several islands. It includes the medieval Old Town, merchants' houses from the 1900s, and many modern factories and offices.

People of the Arctic

The Saami people live in Lapland, a region that extends right across the Scandinavian Arctic. Traditionally they are a nomadic people, who follow their herds of reindeer.

The Little Mermaid

This bronze statue in the Danish capital, Copenhagen, shows a character from one of the children's stories by Hans Christian Andersen (1805-75). Andersen created some of the world's best-loved fairy tales.

N

LOW COUNTRIES

FACT BOX

◆ **Netherlands**
Area: 15,822 sq miles
Population: 15,600,000
Capital: Amsterdam
Official language: Dutch
Currency: Guilder

◆ **Belgium**
Area: 11,732 sq miles
Population: 10,200,000
Capital: Brussels
Official languages: Flemish, French
Currency: Belgian franc

◆ **Luxembourg**
Area: 999 sq miles
Population: 400,000
Capital: Luxembourg
Official language: French, German, Letzebuergesch
Currency: Luxembourg franc

THE COUNTRY OF THE NETHERLANDS is sometimes called Holland, but that is really the name of just two of its provinces, North and South Holland. This is a very flat, low-lying part of northern Europe. Long barriers and sea walls have been built to protect the countryside from North Sea floods. Large areas of land called polders have been reclaimed from the sea over the ages.

1600s by trading with Southeast Asia. Its capital city, Amsterdam, still has many beautiful old houses and canals dating back to this golden age. The Netherlands today remain a center of commerce, exporting bulbs and cut flowers, vegetables, and dairy products, especially cheese, and also electrical goods. Rotterdam is the world's busiest seaport. Peoples of the Netherlands include the Dutch and the Frisians, as well as people whose families came from former Dutch colonies in Indonesia and Suriname.

After a period under Spanish rule, the **Netherlands** became wealthy in the

The Flemish people of **Belgium** are closely related to the Dutch and their two languages are very similar. Belgium is also home to a French-speaking people, the Walloons, who mostly live in the south of the country. Much of the countryside in Belgium is also low and flat, but the land rises to the wooded hills of the Ardennes in the south. The country is heavily industrialized, and is also known for its fine foods— chocolates, pâtés, hams, and traditional beers.

Luxembourg is a tiny country, a survivor of the age when most of Europe was divided into little states, principalities, and duchies. However, modern industry and banking have made Luxembourg wealthy and successful. The people of Luxembourg speak French, German, and a local language called Letzeburgesch.

The three countries have close ties. In 1948, after the terrible years of World War II (1939-1945), Belgium, the Netherlands and Luxembourg set up an economic union called "Benelux." In 1957 they went on to what is now the European Union (EU).

Bruges skyline

The brick gables of old merchants' houses make a pleasing skyline in many historical towns of the Lowlands. Bruges has been famous through the ages for its lacemaking. The city is linked by canal to the seaport of Zeebrugge.

Wetlands butterfly

The Large Copper butterfly is on the endangered species list in both Belgium and the Netherlands. The butterfly thrives in flooded fields. Its caterpillar can survive underwater for many weeks. However, draining of wetlands by farmers and roadbuilders threatens its survival.

NETHERLANDS

Emmen

Groningen   Assen

Almelo   Enschede

Leeuwarden   Meppel

Zwolle

Sneek   North-East Polder

Apeldoorn

Ameland

West Frisian Islands

Terschelling

Vlieland   Wadden Zee   Markerwaard Polder (planned)   Flevoland Polder   Ijssel

Texel   Barrier Dam   IJsselmeer   Amersfoort

Alkmaar   Amsterdam   Hilversum

Zaanstad

Haarlem

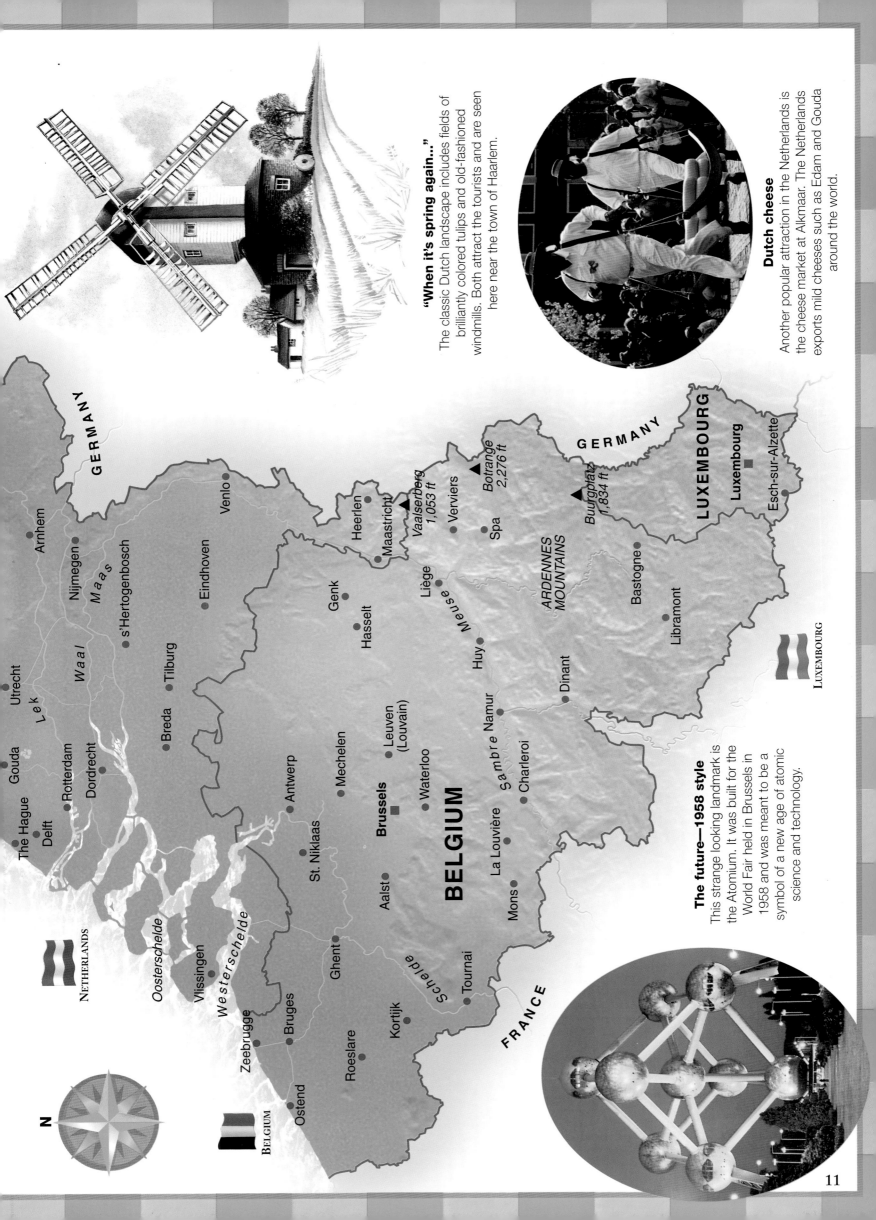

"When it's spring again..."
The classic Dutch landscape includes fields of brilliantly colored tulips and old-fashioned windmills. Both attract the tourists and are seen here near the town of Haarlem.

Dutch cheese
Another popular attraction in the Netherlands is the cheese market at Alkmaar. The Netherlands exports mild cheeses such as Edam and Gouda around the world.

GERMANY

GERMANY

NETHERLANDS

Arnhem
Utrecht
Gouda
The Hague
Delft
Rotterdam
Dordrecht
Nijmegen
s'Hertogenbosch
Breda
Tilburg
Eindhoven
Venlo
Maas
Waal
Lek

Oosterschelde
Westerschelde
Vlissingen
Zeebrugge
Bruges
Ostend
Roeslare
Ghent
St. Niklaas
Antwerp
Mechelen
Kortijk
Tournai
Schelde

Heerlen
Maastricht
Vaalserberg 1,053 ft
Verviers
Spa
Liège
Genk
Hasselt
Meuse
Huy
Namur
Sambre
Dinant
Charleroi
La Louvière
Mons
Waterloo
Leuven (Louvain)
Aalst
Brussels

BELGIUM

Botrange 2,276 ft
ARDENNES MOUNTAINS
Bastogne
Libramont
Buurgplatz 1,834 ft

LUXEMBOURG
Luxembourg
Esch-sur-Alzette

NETHERLANDS

LUXEMBOURG

BELGIUM

FRANCE

N

The future—1958 style
This strange looking landmark is the Atomium. It was built for the World Fair held in Brussels in 1958 and was meant to be a symbol of a new age of atomic science and technology.

BRITISH ISLES

THE BRITISH ISLES lie off the northwestern coast of Europe, between the shallow waters of the North Sea and the stormy Atlantic Ocean. Their western shores are warmed by an ocean current called the North Atlantic Drift. The climate is mild, with a high rainfall in the west.

The largest island is called **Great Britain,** and its three countries (**England, Scotland,** and **Wales**) are joined together within a United Kingdom. The second largest of the British Isles is called **Ireland.** Most of Ireland is an independent republic, but part of the north is governed as a province of the United Kingdom.

Great Britain has a landscape of rolling farmland. There are rugged highlands in Wales and Scotland, while England has rich farmland in the southeast, bleak moors in the north, flat fields in East Anglia, and wild coasts in Cornwall. There are many beautiful old villages and towns, but also large cities and ports.

The Irish landscape is less crowded. It has green fields, misty hills, and, in the west, steep cliffs pounded by Atlantic breakers. Its capital, Dublin, lies on the River Liffey.

English is spoken throughout the British Isles, but other languages may be heard too—Welsh, Irish, and Scots Gaelic, and the various languages spoken by British people of Asian and African descent.

Both the UK and the **Republic of Ireland** are members of the European Union.

Fact Box

Highland games

Scottish pipers parade in the Highland Games. This competition has been taking place since the early nineteenth century, but has its roots in much older clan rivalries.

Wren

One of the most widespread birds of Britain, this short drab colored bird with a cocked tail, has a loud warbling song. Wrens feed on caterpillars, beetles, and bugs.

NORTH SEA

SHETLAND ISLANDS
Unst
Yell
Foula
Lerwick
Sumburgh Head
Fair Isle

ORKNEY ISLANDS
Westray
Hoy
Kirkwall
South Ronaldsay
John o'Groats

SCOTLAND

Cape Wrath
Thurso
Moray Firth
Fraserburgh
Peterhead
Aberdeen
Dee
Don
Spey
Inverness
Loch Ness
NORTH WEST HIGHLANDS
Butt of Lewis
Stornoway
Lewis
North Minch
OUTER HEBRIDES
North Uist
South Uist
Barra
Skye
Rhum
Coll
Tiree
Mull
INNER HEBRIDES
Mallaig
Ben Nevis ▲ 4,405 ft
Oban
Jura
Islay
Kintyre Pen.
GRAMPIAN MTS
Tay
Perth
Loch Lomond
Forth
OCHIL HILLS
SIDLAW HILLS
Dundee
Firth of Forth
Montrose
Edinburgh
Glasgow
Clyde
Greenock
Kilmarnock
Arran
Ayr
Tweed
SOUTHERN UPLANDS
Jedburgh
CHEVIOT HILLS
Berwick-upon-Tweed
St. Abbs Head
Holy I.
SCOTLAND

NORTHERN IRELAND
Malin Head
Tory I.
Rathlin I.
Giants

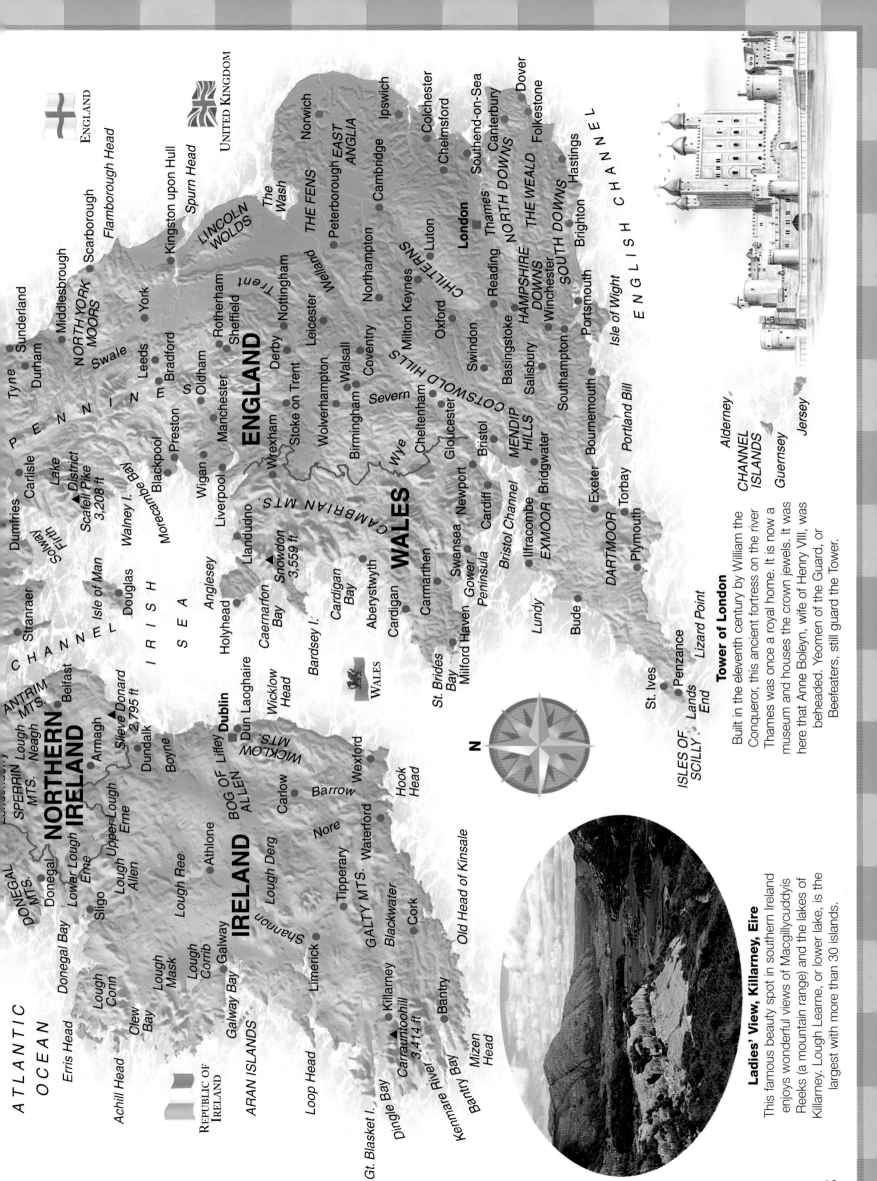

Tower of London

Built in the eleventh century by William the Conqueror, this ancient fortress on the river Thames was once a royal home. It is now a museum and houses the crown jewels. It was here that Anne Boleyn, wife of Henry VIII, was beheaded. Yeomen of the Guard, or Beefeaters, still guard the Tower.

Ladies' View, Killarney, Eire

This famous beauty spot in southern Ireland enjoys wonderful views of Macgillycuddy's Reeks (a mountain range) and the lakes of Killarney. Lough Learne, or lower lake, is the largest with more than 30 islands.

FRANCE AND MONACO

Château de Chaumont
France has many historical castles, palaces and stately homes, or châteaux. Some of the finest are in the Loire valley.

FRANCE IS A LARGE, beautiful country lying at the heart of Western Europe. Its western regions include the massive peaks of the Pyrenees, vineyards and pine forests, peaceful rivers and Atlantic shores.

The north includes the stormy headlands of Brittany, the cliffs of Normandy, and the Channel ports. Rolling fertile plains are drained by the winding river Seine, over whose banks and islands sprawls the French capital. Paris is one of the world's great cities, with broad avenues, historic palaces and churches.

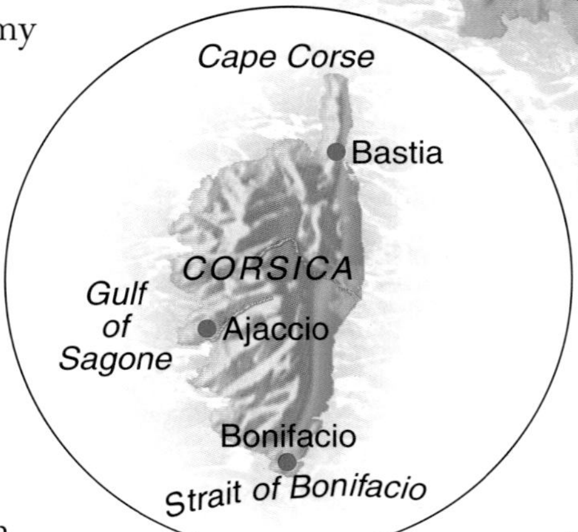
Cape Corse
Bastia
CORSICA
Gulf of Sagone
Ajaccio
Bonifacio
Strait of Bonifacio

The west of **France** is bordered by wooded hills that rise to the high forested slopes of the Jura mountains and finally the spectacular glaciers and ridges of the Alps. The rocks of the Massif Central, shaped by ancient volcanoes, rise in central southern France, to the west of the Rhône valley. The sun-baked hills of southern France border the warm seas of the Mediterranean Sea. This coast includes the wetlands of the Camargue, the great seaport of Marseille, and the fashionable yachting marinas of Cannes.

France has played a major part in history, and the French language is now spoken in many parts of the world. The French people are mostly descended from a Celtic people called the Gauls and Germanic peoples, such as the Franks and Vikings. Within France are several other peoples with their own languages and distinct cultures, such as Bretons, Basques, Catalans, Alsatians, Corsicans, and Algerians.

France is a republic belonging to the European Union (EU) and is an important industrial power, producing cars, aerospace equipment, chemicals, and textiles. The country is renowned for its wines, its cheeses, and its fine cooking.

Part of the Mediterranean coast is occupied by a very small principality called **Monaco**. It has close links with its large neighbor and shares the same currency. The state is famous for its casino.

Cherbourg
Carentan
St. L
Gulf of St-Malo
Granville
Morlaix
St.-Malo
Brest
St-Brieuc
Dinan
Fougeres
Douernenez
Quimper
Pontivy
Rennes
Vitre
Lorient
Vannes
Redon
St. Nazaire
Belle-Ile
Nantes
La Roche-sur-Yon
Isle d'Yeu
Les Sables-d'Olonne
Ré I.
La Rochelle
Rochefor
Oléron I.
Royan
Pauilla
Bayonne
Biarritz
PY
SPAIN

Sacré-Coeur
The gleaming domes of this church soar above the Parisian district of Montmartre, once famed as the haunt of artists and writers.

Shape of the future
The Futuroscope theme park and study center, near Poitiers, is one example of France's many experimental modern buildings. This theatre looks like a huge crystal.

Vineyard harvest
Grapes are gathered at a vineyard in Alsace, on the slopes of the Vosges. Grapes, grown in many regions of France, are made into some of the world's finest wines.

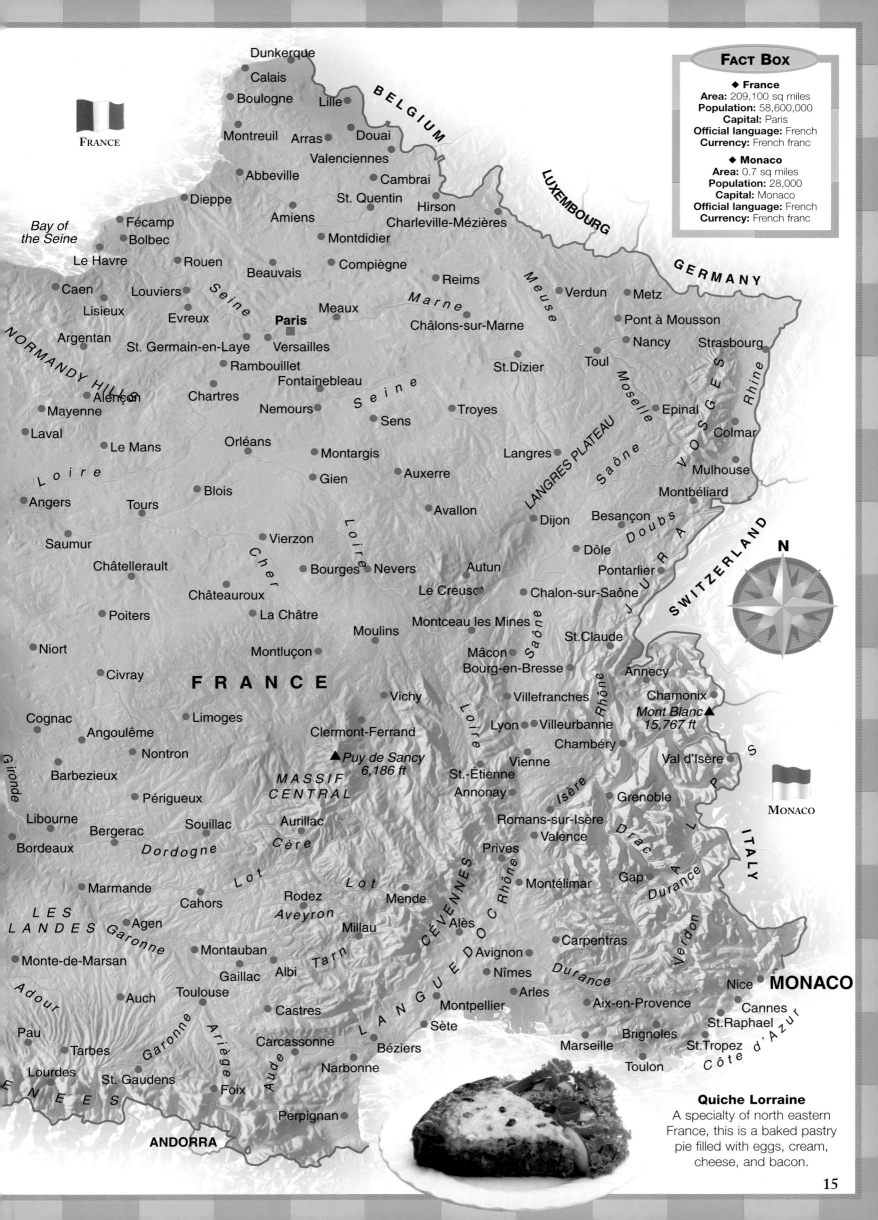

Dunkerque
Calais
Boulogne
Lille
BELGIUM
Montreuil
Arras
Douai
Valenciennes
Abbeville
Cambrai
Dieppe
St. Quentin
Hirson
LUXEMBOURG
Fécamp
Amiens
Charleville-Mézières
Bolbec
Montdidier
Bay of the Seine
GERMANY
Le Havre
Rouen
Compiègne
Reims
Verdun
Metz
Caen
Louviers
Beauvais
Seine
Meuse
Pont à Mousson
Lisieux
Meaux
Châlons-sur-Marne
Marne
Nancy
Strasbourg
Evreux
Paris
Argentan
St. Germain-en-Laye
Versailles
St.Dizier
Toul
NORMANDY HILLS
Alençon
Rambouillet
Fontainebleau
Moselle
Epinal
Mayenne
Chartres
Seine
Troyes
VOSGES
Colmar
Laval
Nemours
Sens
Langres
Rhine
Le Mans
Orléans
Montargis
Auxerre
LANGRES PLATEAU
Mulhouse
Loire
Blois
Gien
Avallon
Saône
Montbéliard
Angers
Tours
Dijon
Besançon
Saumur
Vierzon
Loire
Autun
Dôle
Doubs
Châtellerault
Cher
Bourges
Nevers
Le Creuso
Pontarlier
JURA
Châteauroux
Chalon-sur-Saône
N
Poitiers
La Châtre
Montceau les Mines
St.Claude
SWITZERLAND
Niort
Moulins
Saône
Mâcon
Civray
Montluçon
Bourg-en-Bresse
Annecy
FRANCE
Vichy
Villefranches
Chamonix
Cognac
Limoges
Villeurbanne
Rhône
Mont Blanc 15,767 ft
Angoulême
Clermont-Ferrand
Lyon
Chambéry
Val d'Isère
Nontron
Loire
Vienne
Barbezieux
MASSIF CENTRAL
Puy de Sancy 6,186 ft
St.-Étienne
Isère
Grenoble
Gironde
Périgueux
Annonay
Libourne
Aurillac
Romans-sur-Isère
Bergerac
Souillac
Cère
Valence
Drac
Bordeaux
Dordogne
Prives
ALPS
Marmande
Lot
Lot
Mende
Rhône
Montélimar
Gap
Cahors
Rodez
Durance
LES LANDES
Agen
Garonne
Aveyron
Millau
CÉVENNES
Alès
LANGUEDOC
Carpentras
Verdon
Monte-de-Marsan
Montauban
Tarn
Avignon
Durance
Gaillac
Albi
Nîmes
Nice
MONACO
Pau
Auch
Toulouse
Arles
Aix-en-Provence
Cannes
Adour
Castres
Montpellier
St.Raphael
Garonne
Sète
Brignoles
St.Tropez
Tarbes
Carcassonne
Béziers
Marseille
Côte d'Azur
Lourdes
St. Gaudens
Ariège
Aude
Narbonne
Toulon
PYRENEES
Foix
Perpignan
ANDORRA
ITALY

FRANCE

MONACO

Quiche Lorraine
A specialty of north eastern France, this is a baked pastry pie filled with eggs, cream, cheese, and bacon.

FACT BOX

◆ **Germany**
Area: 137,169 sq miles
Population: 82,000,000
Capital: Berlin
Official language: German
Currency: Deutsche mark

◆ **Switzerland**
Area: 15,870 sq miles
Population: 7,100,000
Capital: Bern
Official languages: German, French, Italian, Romansh
Currency: Swiss franc

◆ **Liechtenstein**
Area: 62 sq miles
Population: 30,000
Capital: Vaduz
Official language: German
Currency: Swiss franc

◆ **Austria**
Area: 32,239 sq miles
Population: 8,100,000
Capital: Vienna
Official language: German
Currency: Schilling

Sylt

NORTH SEA

Flensburg

BALTIC SEA

Kiel Bay

Schleswig

Fehmarn

Rügen

Helgoland

Kiel

Mecklenburg Bay

Stralsund

Rendsburg

Neumünster

Lübeck

Wismar

Rostock

Cuxhaven

Itzehoe

Güstrow

Elmshorn

Norderstedt

Schwerin

Neubrandenburg

Wilhelmshaven

Bremerhaven

Hamburg

Emden

Buxtehude

Müritz Lake

Papenburg

Oldenburg

Bremen

Lüneburg

Neustrelitz

Delmenhorst

Weser

Uelzen

Elbe

Wittenberge

Eberswalde-Finow

Ems

Vechta

Nienburg

Celle

Stendal

Berlin

Nordhorn

Weser

Hannover

Aller

Wolfsburg

Brandenburg

Frankfurt (an der Oder)

Rheine

Osnabrück

Minden

Hildesheim

Brunswick (Braunschweig)

Magdeburg

Potsdam

Gronau

Bielefeld

Hameln

Salzgitter

Eisenhüttenstadt

Münster

TEUTOBURG FOREST

Holzminden

Bad Harzburg

Halberstadt

Dessau

Elbe

Cottbus

Bocholt

Hamm

Paderborn

Göttingen

HARZ MTS.

Halle

Hoyerswerda

Dinslaken

Dortmund

Leine

Nordhausen

Leipzig

Duisburg

Essen

Kassel

Münden

G E R M A N Y

Meissen

Krefeld

Wuppertal

Mühlhausen

Görlitz

Mönchen-Gladbach

Remscheid

Marburg

Erfurt

Weimar

Gera

Dresden

Düsseldorf

Solingen

THURINGIAN FOREST

Jena

Chemnitz

Freiberg

Cologne (Köln)

Bergisch-Gladbach

Zwickau

Aachen

Bonn

Siegen

Alsfeld

Fulda

Suhl

Plauen

CZECH REPUBLIC

Neuwied

Giessen

Fulda

Werra

Hof

Koblenz

Coburg

Daun

Rhine

Wiesbaden

Frankfurt am Main

Schweinfurt

Bayreuth

Mosel

Offenbach

Main

BOHEMIAN FOREST

Trier

Mainz

Würzburg

Bamberg

HUNSRÜCK

Darmstadt

Main

Kitzingen

Saar

Worms

STEIGERWALD

Ludwigshafen

Mannheim

Fürth

Nuremberg (Nürnberg)

Kaiserslautern

Heidelberg

Jagst

Saarbrücken

Karlsruhe

Heilbronn

Regensburg

Pforzheim

Baden-Baden

Stuttgart

Aalen

Ingolstadt

Passau

BLACK FOREST

Tübingen

SWABIAN JURA

Danube

Linz

Rhine

Reutlingen

Ulm

Augsburg

Braunau

Wels

Steyr

Freiburg

Neckar

Munich (München)

Inn

Memmingen

Lech

Rosenheim

Gmunden

Salzburg

Schaffhausen

Konstanz

Kempten

Hallein

Winterthur

Lake Constance (Bodensee)

Kufstein

AUSTRIA

Basel

Baden

St Gallen

Salzach

Solothurn

Zurich

LIECHTENSTEIN

Zugspitze 9,717 ft

Kitzbühel

Neuchâtel

Lucerne

Zug

Vaduz

Innsbruck

NIEDERE TAUERN

Bern

Inn

Brenner

HOHE TAUERN

Mur

Lake Neuchâtel

Fribourg

SWITZERLAND

Chur

Davos

Grossglockner 9,391 ft

Wolfsberg

Lausanne

Thun

Interlaken

Andermatt

Klagenfurt

Lake Geneva

Montreux

ITALY

Villach

Drava

Thonon

St Moritz

Geneva

BERNESE ALPS

LEPONTINE ALPS

Locarno

Bellinzona

SLOVENIA

Martigny

Zermatt

Lugano

Matterhorn 14,688 ft

Monte Rosa 15,120 ft

BELGIUM

LUXEMBOURG

FRANCE

N

GERMANY

SWITZERLAND

LIECHTENSTEIN

AUSTRIA

Oder

Neisse

POLAND

Mörfelden

16

GERMANY & THE ALPS

GERMANY LIES BETWEEN Western and Central Europe. In the south the high peaks of the Alps are flanked by belts of forest.

The rolling hills and heathland of the center stretch to the North Sea, while in the west the rivers Rhine and Moselle wind through steep valleys planted with vines. In the northeast a vast plain is bordered by the Baltic Sea and by the rivers Oder and Neisse.

For most of its history Germany has been divided into different states. Today's united Germany dates from 1990. Germany is a federal republic, which means that its regions or Länder have considerable powers. The country is a leading member of the European Union and is a major world producer of cars, electrical and household goods, medicines, chemicals, wines, and beers.

Switzerland is a small country set among the lakes and snowy peaks of the Alps and the Jura ranges. Its beautiful landscape and historical towns attract many tourists. Industries include dairy produce, precision instruments, and finance. Zurich is a world center of banking, while Geneva is the headquarters of many international agencies, such as the Red Cross and the World Health Organization.

To the east is the tiny country of **Liechtenstein,** which is closely linked with Switzerland and uses the same currency. The land of **Austria** descends from the soaring peaks of the Alps to the flat lands of the Danube river valley. Austria once ruled a large empire which stretched eastward into Hungary and southward into Italy. Today Austria still plays an important part in Europe, making its living from tourism, farming, forestry, and manufacture.

German is spoken through most of the region, with a great variety of dialects. In parts of Switzerland there are people who speak French, Italian, and Romansh.

Krems
Danube **Vienna**
St Pölten
Bruck
Baden
Neusiedler See
Wiener Neustadt
Kapfenberg
Leoben
Graz
HUNGARY

Edelweiss
This small herb, with its pretty white flower, grows in the European Alps. High mountain meadows are filled with wildflowers in spring and summer.

Brimming with beer
Munich, capital of Bavaria in southern Germany, hosts a famous beer festival every October. Regional dress is still common in the region.

River of ice
This impressive glacier grinds its way down the Alps near Zermatt. Many tourists and climbers visit Switzerland to enjoy the spectacular views.

Medieval revelry
Festival costumes recall the Middle Ages in Baden Württemberg. During that period Germany was made up of many small states.

IBERIAN PENINSULA

THE IBERIAN PENINSULA is in southwestern Europe, and juts out into the Atlantic Ocean. It is bordered to the north by the stormy Bay of Biscay and to the south by the Mediterranean Sea and the Balearic Islands. Across the Strait of Gibraltar, just 8 miles away, lies the continent of Africa.

The north coast, green from high rainfall, rises to the Cantabrian mountains, while the snowy Pyrenees form a high barrier along the Spanish-French frontier. Another range, the Sierra Nevada, runs parallel with the south coast. Inland, much of the Iberian peninsula is taken up by an extremely dry, rocky plateau, which swelters in the heat of summer. To the west are forested highlands and the fertile plains of Portugal, crossed by great rivers such as the Douro, Tagus and Guadiana.

The Iberian peninsula is occupied by four countries or territories. There is **Gibraltar**, a British colony since 1713, and the tiny independent state of **Andorra**, high in the Pyrenees. The two main countries of the region are **Spain** and **Portugal**. Both have a history of overseas settlement, and both Spanish and Portuguese have become the chief languages of Latin America. Many people speak other languages, including Basque and Catalan, and have their own traditions and history.

Both Spain and Portugal were ruled by dictators for much of the 20th century, but today both are democracies and members of the European Union. Spain produces olives, citrus fruits, wines, and sherries, and has a large fishing fleet. Portugal also produces wine and port takes its name from the city of Oporto. Fishing villages line the coasts and cork, used for bottle stoppers and tiling, is cut from the thick bark of the cork oak tree.

PORTUGAL

Map labels:

N

Bay of Biscay
Cape Ortegal
Cape Peñas
La Coruña · El Ferrol · Gijón · Llanes
Carballo · Villalba · Oviedo
Cape Finisterre · Lugo · Fonsagrada · CANTABRIAN
Santiago de Compostela · Sarria · Sil
Lalin · León
Monforte de Lemos · Astorga
Vigo · Miño · Orense · SIERRA CABRERA · Villada
La Gudina · Esla
Baltar · Bragança
Braga · Tâmega · Tuela · Valladolid
Mogadouro · Zamora
Vila Real · Medina del Campo
Porto · Douro · Tormes
Lamego · Salamanca
PORTUGAL
Aviero · Viseu · Cuidad Rodrigo · Avila
Guarda · Béjar
Coimbra · Covilhã · SIERRA DE GREDOS
Plasencia · Tajo
Castelo Branco
Leiria · Cáceres · Trujillo
Tomar
Caldas da Rainha · Tagus · Portalegre
Santarém
Lisbon · Badajoz · Don Benito
Almendralejo
Setúbal · Évora
Pozoblanco
Ardila · Azuaga · SIERRA
Beja · Córdoba
Guadiana · Chança · Constantina
Nerva · Guadalquivir
Huelva · Seville · Puente Genil
Lagos · Osuna
Faro · Costa de la Luz · Morón de la Frontera
Cape Saint Vincent · Algarve · Gulf of Cadiz · Ronda
Jerez de la Frontera
Cádiz · SIERRA DE RONDA · Marbella
Gibraltar (U.K.)
Algeciras
Strait of Gibraltar
Cueta (Spain)

Feria in Seville
At the Feria, held in the Spanish city of Seville every April, people ride into town dressed in traditional finery. The river is lined with tents and pavilions. The festival is celebrated with bullfights, flamenco music, and dancing.

Fishing boats, Nazaré
Fishing boats line the beach at Nazaré, on the Portuguese coast. The fishermen brave the Atlantic waves daily in their search for the sardines and tuna that make up their catch.

Santander
Bilbao
San Sebastián
MOUNTAINS
Reinosa
Vitoria
Pamplona
FRANCE
PYRENEES
ANDORRA
Pico de Aneto 11,165 ft
Andorra la Vella
Figueras
Osorno
Burgos
Logroño
Ebro
Arga
Gállego
Cinca
Llobregat
Gerona
Manresa
Costa Brava
Palencia
Duero
Soria
Ebro
Saragossa
Lérida
Tarrasa
Costa Dorada
Barcelona
S P A I N
Jalón
Reus
Tarragona
Segovia
SIERRA DE GUADARRAMA
Tajuña
Tajo
Caspe
Tortosa
Cape Tortosa
ANDORRA
Guadalajara
Alcalá de Henares
Morella
Vinaroz
Costa del Azahar
Teruel
Mijares
Menorca
Mallorca
Mahón
Madrid
Cuenca
Castellón de la Plana
Turia
SPAIN
Palma
Manacor
Aranjuez
Sagunto
Toledo
MONTES E TOLEDO
Requena
Júcar
Valencia
Gulf of Valencia
B A L E A R I C I S L A N D S
Villarrobledo
Alcira
Ibiza
Daimiel
Manzanares
Albacete
Ibiza
Formentera
Ciudad Real
Guadiana
Almansa
Cape Neo
Valdepeñas
Alcaraz
Alcoy
Yecla
Portuguese explorers
Puertollano
LORENA
SIERRA DE SEGURA
Alicante
Elche
Costa Blanca
This monument is in Lisbon, the Portuguese capital. It honors the Portuguese seafarers who were among the first Europeans to explore the coasts of Africa, Asia, and the Americas. Prince Henry (1394–1460) founded the first school of navigation.
La Carolina
Moratalla
Segura
Orihuela
Linares
Cehegín
Murcia
Jaén
Lorca
Cartagena
Cape Palos
Martos
Baza
Aguilas
Guadix
Huércal Overa
Genil
Granada
Costa Blanca
Mulhacén 11,408 ft
SIERRA NEVADA
Almería
Antequera
Málaga
Motril
Berja
Cape Gata
Costa del Sol
M E D I T E R R A N E A N   S E A

Spanish paella
Paella takes its name from the large pan in which it is cooked. It is made of rice with saffron and garlic, mixed with shrimp and other seafoods, vegetables, chicken, or ham.

Melilla (Spain)

ITALY AND ITS NEIGHBORS

ITALY OCCUPIES a long, boot-shaped peninsula that stretches south from the snowy peaks and blue lakes of the Alps into the Mediterranean Sea. The country also takes in the large islands of Sardinia and Sicily. The northern regions of the mainland include the wide, fertile plains around the river Po and wealthy industrial cities.

A long chain of mountains, the Appenines, run down the spine of **Italy**. They descend to coastal farmland and the hot, dry plains of the south. Southern Italy and its islands are one of the world's volcanic danger zones. Olives and grapes grow well in its sunny climate and Italy is the largest wine producer in the world. Factories produce automobiles, textiles, and leather goods.

Modern Italy has only been united since 1861, but in ancient times Rome was the capital of a vast empire stretching across western Europe, southwest Asia, and North Africa. Rome later became the center of the Catholic Church and during the 1400s and 1500s cities such as Florence saw a great flowering of scholarship and the arts, known as the Renaissance. Many tourists visit Italy to see its ancient sites.

Italian, based on the ancient Latin language, is spoken throughout Italy, but in border regions you may hear other languages—French, German, or Slovenian. The Ladin language is spoken in the Dolomite mountains and the people of Sardinia speak their own ancient dialect of Italian.

Two small independent states lie entirely surrounded by Italian territory. One is the world's smallest country, known as **Vatican City**. It is a district of Rome which serves as headquarters for the Pope and the Roman Catholic Church. The other is tiny **San Marino.**

South of Italy, toward the coast of North Africa is the chain of islands that make up **Malta.** The Maltese have their own language and live from building and repairing ships and from tourism.

Sun and sea

Portofino is a small town on the Gulf of Genoa, in Italy's Liguria region. Its pretty waterfront and fishing boats attract many tourists in the hot Mediterranean summer.

Spaghetti Bolognese

Spaghetti is a kind of pasta. Made from wheat and eggs, pasta is eaten in all kinds of shapes and sizes, each with its own name. Here it is served with a meat and tomato sauce, invented in the city of Bologna. Italians who have left their homeland have made their cooking popular around the world.

SLOVENIA

AUSTRIA

SWITZERLAND

Trieste
Udine
Portogruaro
Venice
Piave
Chioggia
Treviso
Comacchio
Bolzano
Borgo
Vicenza
Padua
Ravenna
Adria
Rimini
Trento
Verona
Ferrara
Reno
Forlì
L. Garda
Mantova
Po
Bologna
San Marino
Brescia
Carpi
Panaro
Modena
Bergamo
Oglio
Parma
Reggio nell'Emilia
Lecco
Monza
Cremona
Piacenza
Pistoia
L. Como
Milan
Pavia
Lodi
Carrara
Lucca
Florence
L. Maggiore
Massa
Arno
Alessandra
Viareggio
Ticino
Novi Ligure
La Spezia
Pisa
Biella
Genoa
Livorno
Turin
Savona
Gulf of Genoa
Tanaro
Cuneo

PESARO
SAN MARINO
Ancona
Iesi
Macerata
Gubbio
San Benedetto
N
Arezzo
Perugia
N
Teramo
Cortona
L. Trasimeno
I T A L Y
Siena
L. Bolsena
Terni
Piombino
Grosseto
Elba
Capraia

LIGURIAN SEA

MONACO

FRANCE

Mont Blanc 15,767 ft
Monte Rosa 15,120 ft

VATICAN CITY

ITALY

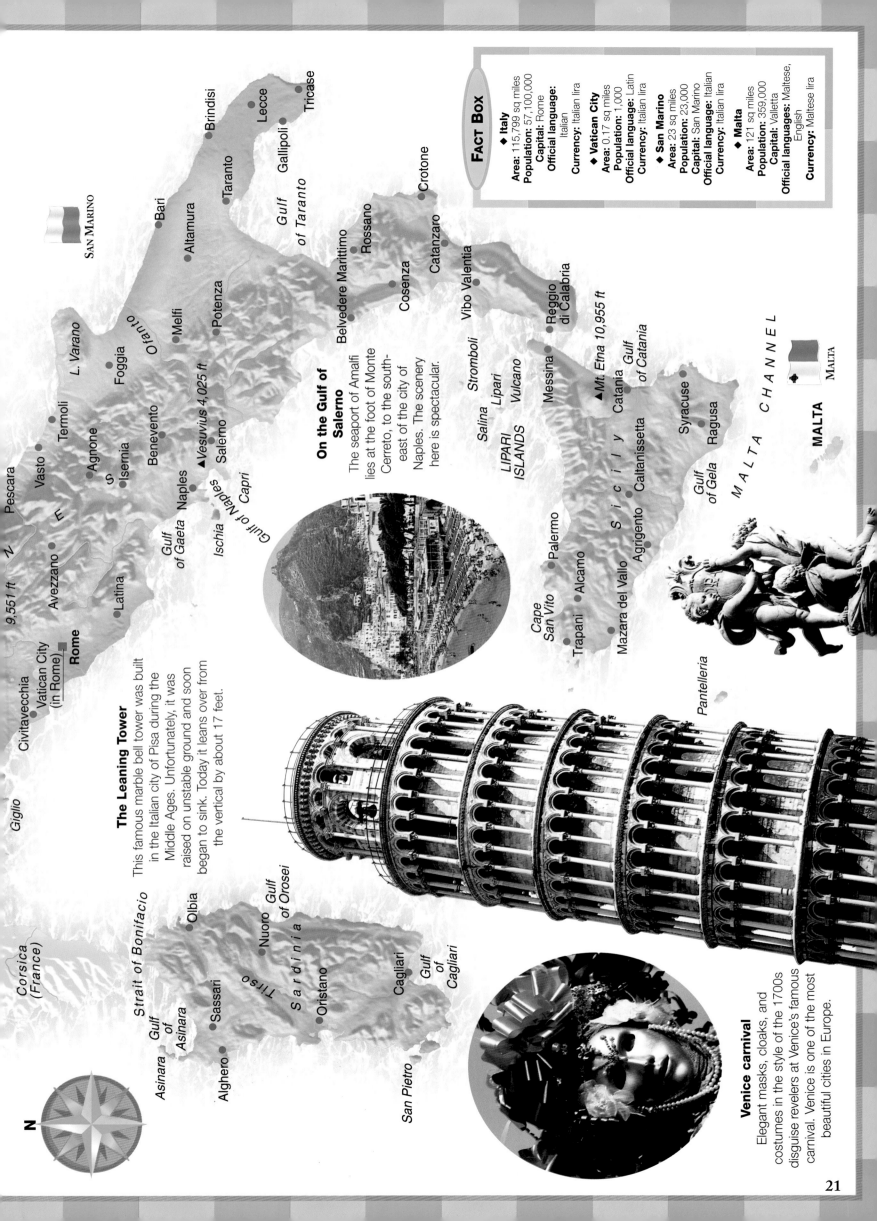

N

9,551 ft

Corsica
(France)

Strait of Bonifacio

Asinara Gulf
of
Asinara

Alghero ● Sassari

Tirso

Nuoro Gulf
of Orosei

Sardinia

Olbia ●

Oristano ●

Cagliari
Gulf
of
Cagliari

San Pietro

The Leaning Tower
This famous marble bell tower was built in the Italian city of Pisa during the Middle Ages. Unfortunately, it was raised on unstable ground and soon began to sink. Today it leans over from the vertical by about 17 feet.

Venice carnival
Elegant masks, cloaks, and costumes in the style of the 1700s disguise revelers at Venice's famous carnival. Venice is one of the most beautiful cities in Europe.

Giglio

Civitavecchia

Vatican City
(in Rome) ■ **Rome**

Pescara

● Vasto

● Avezzano

● Latina

● Termoli

Agnone ●

● Isernia

S

E

L. Varano

Foggia ●

Benevento ●

Melfi ●

Potenza ●

Ofanto

▲Vesuvius 4,025 ft

Naples Salerno

Gulf
of Gaeta

Ischia

Gulf of Naples

Gulf of Capri

SAN MARINO

Bari ●

Altamura ●

Taranto ●

● Brindisi

● Lecce

Gallipoli

Tricase

Gulf
of Taranto

On the Gulf of Salerno
The seaport of Amalfi lies at the foot of Monte Cerreto, to the southeast of the city of Naples. The scenery here is spectacular.

Belvedere Marittimo

● Rossano

● Cosenza

● Crotone

Catanzaro

Vibo Valentia

Reggio
di Calabria

Stromboli

Salina Lipari

Vulcano

LIPARI
ISLANDS

Messina

▲Mt. Etna 10,955 ft

Catania Gulf
of Catania

Sicily

Caltanissetta

Syracuse

Ragusa

Gulf
of Gela

Palermo ●

Alcamo ●

Cape
San Vito ●

Trapani ●

Mazara del Vallo ●

Agrigento ●

Pantelleria

MALTA CHANNEL

MALTA

MALTA

CENTRAL EUROPE

THREE SMALL COUNTRIES cluster around the eastern shores of the Baltic Sea. **Estonia, Latvia,** and **Lithuania** were part of the Soviet Union (today's Russian Federation) from 1940 until 1991, when they became independent. Their lands include forests and lakes, farmland and industrial cities.

Poland, which has historic links with Lithuania, is a large country which has also known invasions and foreign rule through much of its history. Despite this, the Poles, a Slavic people, have kept a sense of independence and a pride in their traditions. The lands near Poland's Baltic coast are dotted with lakes. The north is a flat land of pine forests, part of the great plain which stretches from eastern Germany into Russia. It is cold and snowy in winter, but warm in summer. In southern Poland the land rises to highlands and the jagged peaks of the Tatra mountains, along the Slovakian border.

Slovakia and the **Czech Republic** were a single country until 1993. Slovakia is a land of high mountains dropping to fertile farmland around the River Danube, which forms its southeastern border. When the two countries divided, most industry lay on the Czech side of the border. The Czech Republic produces beer, glass, ceramics, steel, and machinery. The country is bordered by mountains and, in the east, by the Bohemian center of learning and the arts.

The Czechs and Slovaks are both Slavic peoples, but the Hungarians are Magyars, a people who invaded and settled in the region about 1200 years ago. **Hungary** is a country of wide open plains and low mountains. Its fertile farmland produces fruits, grains, and grapes for making strong red wine. Its beautiful capital, Budapest, is on the River Danube.

Historical Prague

Prague, capital of the Czech Republic, is a fine old city on the River Vltava. Prague was the chief city of independent Bohemia in the Middle Ages.

FACT BOX

◆ **Poland**
  Area: 120,196 sq miles
  Population: 38,600,000
  Capital: Warsaw
  Official language: Polish
  Currency: Zloty

◆ **Czech Republic**
  Area: 30,315 sq miles
  Population: 10,330,000
  Capital: Prague
  Official language: Czech
  Currency: Koruna

◆ **Slovakia**
  Area: 18,849 sq miles
  Population: 5,400,000
  Capital: Bratislava
  Official language: Slovak
  Currency: Koruna

◆ **Hungary**
  Area: 35,762 sq miles
  Population: 10,294,000
  Capital: Budapest
  Official language: Hungarian
  Currency: Forint

◆ **Latvia**
  Area: 24,486 sq miles
  Population: 2,700,000
  Capital: Riga
  Official language: Latvian
  Currency: Lats

◆ **Lithuania**
  Area: 25,063 sq miles
  Population: 3,742,000
  Capital: Kiev
  Official language: Vilnius
  Currency: Litas

◆ **Estonia**
  Area: 16,183 sq miles
  Population: 1,517,000
  Capital: Tallinn
  Official language: Estonian
  Currency: Kroon

ESTONIA

LATVIA

LITHUANIA

POLAND

RUSSIA

Lake Peipus

Kohtla-Järve

Tartu

Munamagi 1,043 ft ▲

ESTONIA

Parnu

Hiumaa

Saaremaa

Tallinn

Gaizina 1,020 ft ▲

LATVIA

Gulf of Riga

Riga

Jurmala

Ventspils

Saldus

Jelgava

Liepāja

Daugavpils

Utena

Ukmerge

Vilnius

1,026 ft ▲

Panevezys

LITHUANIA

Siauliai

Kaunas

Nemunas (Neman)

Klaipeda

Kaliningrad (RUSSIA)

Gulf of Gdansk

Gdynia

Gdansk

Kaliningrad

N

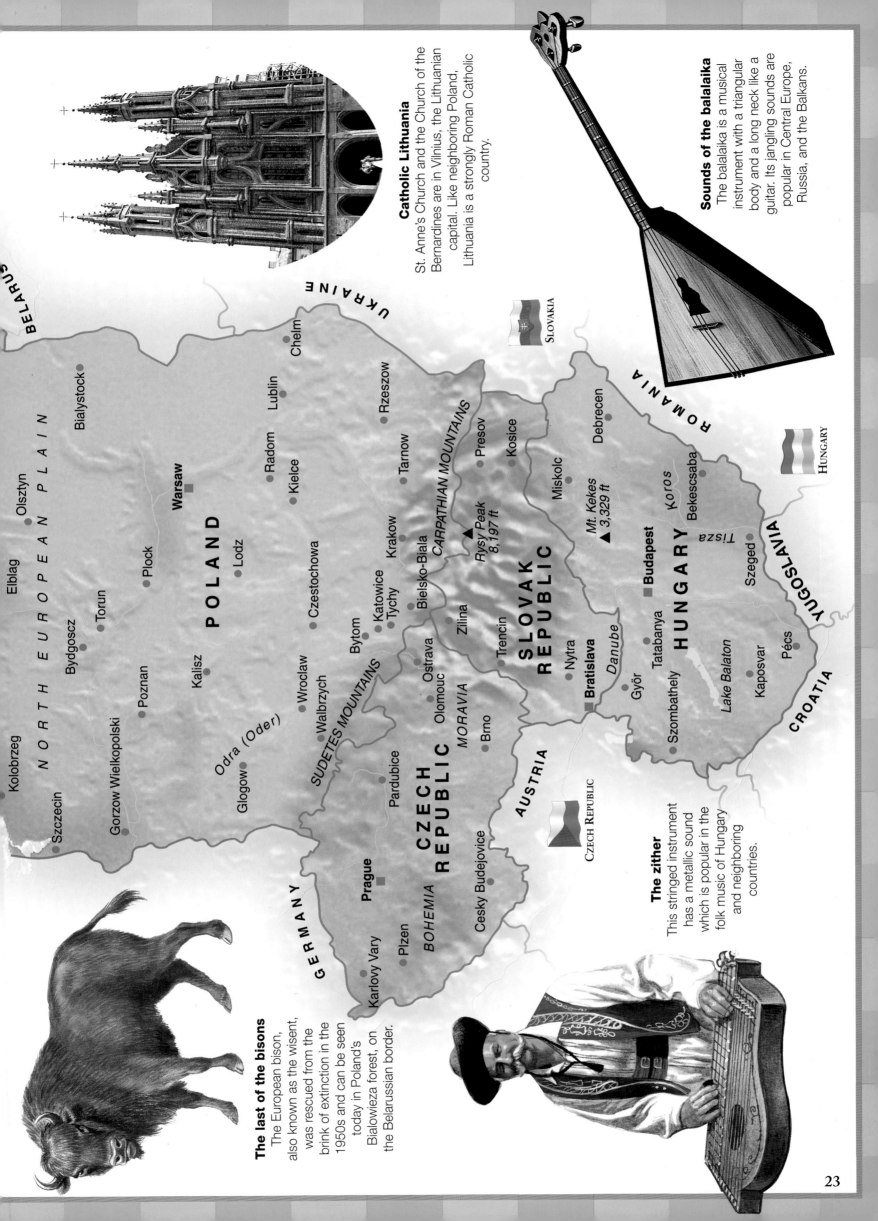

Catholic Lithuania
St. Anne's Church and the Church of the Bernardines are in Vilnius, the Lithuanian capital. Like neighboring Poland, Lithuania is a strongly Roman Catholic country.

Sounds of the balalaika
The balalaika is a musical instrument with a triangular body and a long neck like a guitar. Its jangling sounds are popular in Central Europe, Russia, and the Balkans.

BELARUS

UKRAINE

SLOVAKIA

ROMANIA

HUNGARY

Chelm

Bialystock

Lublin

Radom

Rzeszow

Presov

Kosice

Debrecen

Miskolc

N O R T H   E U R O P E A N   P L A I N

Olsztyn

Elblag

Kielce

Tarnow

CARPATHIAN MOUNTAINS

Koros

Bekescsaba

Warsaw

Krakow

Rysy Peak
8,197 ft

Mt. Kekes
▲ 3,329 ft

Budapest

Tisza

Szeged

Plock

Lodz

P O L A N D

Czestochowa

Bielsko-Biala

Katowice
Tychy

Zilina

S L O V A K
R E P U B L I C

HUNGARY

Kolobrzeg

Bydgoscz

Torun

Poznan

Kalisz

Bytom

Trencin

Nytra

Bratislava

Danube

Györ

Tatabanya

Szombathely

Lake Balaton

Kaposvar

Pécs

YUGOSLAVIA

Szczecin

Gorzow Wielkopolski

Wroclaw

Walbrzych

Ostrava

Olomouc

MORAVIA

Brno

AUSTRIA

CZECH REPUBLIC

CROATIA

Glogow

Odra (Oder)

SUDETES MOUNTAINS

C Z E C H
R E P U B L I C

Pardubice

G E R M A N Y

B O H E M I A

Prague

Cesky Budejovice

Karlovy Vary

Plzen

The last of the bisons
The European bison, also known as the wisent, was rescued from the brink of extinction in the 1950s and can be seen today in Poland's Bialowieza forest, on the Belarussian border.

The zither
This stringed instrument has a metallic sound which is popular in the folk music of Hungary and neighboring countries.

BALKANS AND ROMANIA

THE STATES OF SOUTHERN Central Europe are known as the Balkans. They take their name from the Balkan peninsula, a great wedge of land that stretches south into the Mediterranean.

The warm, blue waters around the Balkan coast form the Adriatic, Aegean, and Black Seas and are popular with tourists. The region is mountainous, with hot, dry summers. Winters are severe in the north of the region, but generally mild in the south. Earthquakes are common. The Balkan countries produce fruit, wines and liquor, dairy products such as yogurt and cheese, olives, sunflowers, and tobacco.

In the early 1990s the northwest of the region saw bitter fighting as the large nation of Yugoslavia broke up into separate independent states. These took the names of **Slovenia**, **Croatia**, **Bosnia-Herzegovina**, **Yugoslavia** (Serbia and Montenegro), and **Macedonia** (which is also the name of the northernmost province of Greece). The small and very poor country of **Albania** also suffered from political unrest and civil war in the 1990s.

The northeast of the Balkan peninsula is occupied by **Bulgaria**, a land of fertile farmland to the south of the river Danube, crossed by the Balkan and Rhodope mountain chains. Its northern neighbor is **Romania**, lying around the forested Carpathian mountain range and the Transylvanian Alps. On the Black Sea coast, the river Danube forms a marshy delta region.

The Balkan peninsula narrows to the south, breaking up into the headland of the Peloponnese and scattered island chains. **Greece** was the center of Europe's first great civilizations, between 4,000 and 2,000 years ago. The rock of the Acropolis, with its temple, the Parthenon, still towers above the Greek capital, Athens.

The sunflower crop
Sunflowers are grown in many parts of southern Europe. Their seeds may be roasted and eaten as snacks, turned into cooking oil or used to make margarine.

Off to market
Romanian farmers gather for a cattle fair at Sugatag. The population as a whole is made up of Romanians, whose language is linked to the Latin language of the ancient Roman empire, as well as Magyars and Gypsies.

Old-fashioned style
Traditional Bulgarian costumes, with waistcoats, aprons and skirts may still be seen at many festivals or folk dances.

UKRAINE

ROMANIA

MOLDOVA

Satu Mare
Baia Mare
Oradea
Cluj-Napoca
Somes
Mures
Tîrgu Mures
Botosani
Iasi
Bacau
Siret

MOLDAVIAN CARPATHIANS

HUNGARY

Arad
Alba Iulia
ROMANIA
Mures
Timisoara
Deva
Sibiu
Brasov
*Moldoveanu▲
8,341 ft*
Galati
Braila

Subotica
VOJVODINA
Resita
TRANSYLVANIAN ALPS
Ploiesti
Pitesti

Osijek
Novi Sad
Belgrade
Jiu
Craiova
Bucharest
Constanta

Brcko
uzla
Sabac
Smederevo
Negotin
Dunarea (Danube)
Ruse
Dobrich
DOBRUJA

Valjevo
Kragujevac
Vidin
Iskur
Pleven
Shumen
Balchik

Srebrenica
Cacak
Morava
Mikhaylovgrad
Vratsa
Lovech
Turgovishte
Kamchiya
Varna

Drina
Krusevac
Nis
BALKAN MOUNTAINS
Sofia
Kazanluk
Sliven
Burgas

Novi Pazar
SERBIA
Leskovac
Pernik
Pasardzhik
Maritsa
Stara Zagora
Yambol

YUGOSLAVIA
Pristina
*Musala Peak
9,594 ft ▲*
Plovdiv
Khaskovo

ONTENEGRO
Pec
KOSOVO
Urosevac
BULGARIA
Tundzha

Podgorica
Lake Scutari
Skopje
Struma
Smolyan
Orestiás

nkodër
*Mt Korabit ▲
9,023 ft*
Tetovo
MACEDONIA
RHODOPE MOUNTAINS
Drama
Komotiní

*Drin
Gulf*
Durrës
Tiranë
Prilep
Vardar
PIRIN MTS
Xánthi

Elbasan
Lake Ohrid
Bitola
Palikastron
Sérrai
Kaválla
Alexandroúpolis

Lake Prespa
Edhessa
Kilkís
Thásos

ALBANIA
Náousa
Thessaloníki
Samothrace

Vlore
Ptolemaïs
Aliakmon
Límnos

Gjirokaster
*Mt Olympus
▲ 9,568 ft*
*Mt Áthos
6,668 ft ▲*

GREECE
Ioánnina
Trikkala
Lárisa
Vólos
Mitilíni

Kérkira
Corfu
Párga
PINDUS MTS.
Skíathos
Lesbos

Arta
Akhelóos
Kardhítsa
Skópelos
Skíros

Pálairos
Lamia
Euboea
*AEGEAN
SEA*

Leukas
Astakós
Agrínion
*Parnassus
▲ 8,354 ft*
Kími
Khalkís
Chios

Cephalonia
Ithaca
Pátrai
Marathon
Ándros
Sámos

*IONIAN
SEA*
Amaliás
Lambía
Corinth
Mégara
Athens
Tínos
Ikaria

Zante
Alfíos
Argos
Piraeus
Láyrion
Kéa

Pírgos
Tripolis
Návplion
Kíthnos
Síros
Míkonos
Pátmos

PELOPONNESUS
Galatás
Sérifos
Páros
Léros

Kalamáta
Sparta
Sífnos
Náxos
Kálimnos

Cos

Areópolis
Mílos
Íos
Astipálaia

Neápolis
Thíra
Tílos
Rhodes

Cythera
Rhodes
Líndos

SEA OF CRETE
Kárpathos

Khaniá
Réthimnon
Iráklion
Crete
*Mt. Ida
8,056 ft*

Islands from volcanoes

The Greek island of Santorini (or Thira) is one of the islands that form the Cyclades in the Aegean Sea. Once a volcano, the island has steep cliffs and narrow, winding streets. It has become a popular destination for tourists.

FACT BOX

◆ **Slovenia**
Area: 7,784 sq miles
Population: 1,990,000
Capital: Ljublana
Official language: Slovenian
Currency: Tolar

◆ **Croatia**
Area: 21,734 sq miles
Population: 4,789,000
Capital: Zagreb
Official language: Serbo-Croat
Currency: Croatian dinar

◆ **Bosnia-Herzegovina**
Area: 19,654 sq miles
Population: 4,366,000
Capital: Sarajevo
Official language: Serbo-Croat
Currency: Bosnian dinar

◆ **Yugoslavia (Serbia-Montenegro)**
Area: 39,274 sq miles
Population: 10,600,000
Capital: Belgrade
Official language: Serbo-Croat
Currency: Dinar

◆ **Macedonian (former Yugoslav) Republic**
Area: 9,885 sq miles
Population: 2,173,000
Capital: Skopje
Official language: Macedonian
Currency: Dinar

◆ **Albania**
Area: 11,052 sq miles
Population: 3,363,000
Capital: Tiranë
Official language: Albanian
Currency: Lek

◆ **Romania**
Area: 91,295 sq miles
Population: 22,767,000
Capital: Bucharest
Official language: Romanian
Currency: Leu

◆ **Bulgaria**
Area: 42,630 sq miles
Population: 8,469,000
Capital: Sofia
Official language: Bulgarian
Currency: Lev

◆ **Greece**
Area: 50,735 sq miles
Population: 10,500,000
Capital: Athens
Official language: Greek
Currency: Drachma

Clear waters

A waterfall sparkles in the sunshine in Croatia. This is a small country of many landscapes.

RUSSIA AND ITS NEIGHBORS

FOR A LARGE PART OF THIS CENTURY all the countries on this map were part of one huge country, the Soviet Union. That nation was formed in the years after November 1917, when communists seized power from the czars. Communist rule ended in 1991 and many of the regions around the former Soviet borders then broke away to become independent countries.

St. Basil's Cathedral, Russia
Moscow is famous for the onion-shaped domes of St. Basil's Cathedral. It was built in 1555 by Czar Ivan IV to commemorate the defeat of invading Tartars.

The remaining part of the former Soviet Union was renamed the "**Russian Federation.**" It is still by far the largest country in the world, stretching across two continents, Europe and Asia. Eighty percent of the population are Russians, but the rest belong to one of the many other ethnic groups who live in this enormous region.

Northern Russia is a land of tundra, where deep-frozen soil borders the Arctic Ocean. To the south is the great belt of forest known as taiga, whose spruce trees are heavy with snow during the long, bitter winter. Southern Russia and the **Ukraine** have the fertile black earth of the rolling grasslands known as steppes. The lands to the south of Russia's new borders take in warm, fertile valleys, thin grasslands grazed by sheep and goats, deserts, and high mountains.

Russia is rich in minerals, oil, natural gas, and timber. Its industries were developed in a hurry during the Soviet years, but at great cost to its people and environment. Russia is still an economic giant, producing machinery, textiles, chemicals, and vehicles.

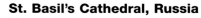

Franz Josef Land

FINLAND

BELARUS

LITHUANIA

RUSSIA

ESTONIA

LATVIA

Murmansk · *BARENTS SEA* · *Novaya Zemlya* · *KARA SEA*

L. Ladoga

Archangel · Amderma · Dikson

St. Petersburg · L. Onega · *N. Dvina* · *Pechora* · Salekhard · *Yenisey*

BELARUS

Minsk · Smolensk · Yaroslavl' · Kirov · *SIBERIAN LOWLAND*

Gomel

UKRAINE

Chernobyl

Moscow · *Volga* · Khanty-Mansiysk

UKRAINE ■ **Kiev** · Nizhniy Novgorod · Kazan · *Kama* · Perm · Nizhniy Tagil · *Irtysh* · *Ob'* · *Yenisey*

MOLDOVA · *Dnepr* · Voronezh · Syzran · Ufa · Tobol'sk

Chisinau · Khar'kov · Saratov · Samara · Yekaterinburg

Odessa · Donetsk · *Don* · *Volga* · Chelyabinsk

Sevastopol · Volgograd · Magnitogorsk · *Ural* · Omsk · Tomsk

BLACK SEA · Rostov-on-Don · Orsk · Novosibirsk

Mt. Elbrus 18,506 ft · Astrakhan · *Ishim* · *Irtysh* · Aqmola

MOLDOVA · Groznyy · *Caspian Sea* · Karaganda

Batumi · *CAUCASUS MTS* · **K A Z A K H S T A N** · Semey · *SAYAN*

TURKEY · **GEORGIA Tbilisi** · *Aral Sea* · Balkhash

ARMENIA · *Syr Darya* · *TURANIAN PLATEAU* · *Lake Balkhash* · *CHINA*

GEORGIA · **Yerevan** · **AZERBAIJAN** · Nukus · Almaty

AZER. · Tashauz

Baku · **UZBEKISTAN** · **Bishkek KYRGYZSTAN**

ARMENIA · **TURKMENISTAN** · Bukhara · **Tashkent**

Ashgabat · *Amu Darya* · **Dushanbe** · KYRGYZSTAN

UZBEKISTAN · I R A N · **TAJIKISTAN**

AZERBAIJAN · TURKMENISTAN · AFGHANISTAN · TAJIKISTAN

R U S S I A

URAL MOUNTAINS · *Ob'*

Coarse cotton
Cotton of a tough, coarse grade is grown in Uzbekistan. The country is a major world producer, but in this dry land the cotton crop needs a great deal of irrigation, and this has harmed the environment.

Happy Easter!
Many Russians are Christians belonging to the Eastern Orthodox Church. Traditionally, they exchanged beautifully decorated eggs as gifts at Easter.

RUSSIA

Wrangel I.

EAST SIBERIAN SEA

Anadyr'

Severnaya Zemlya

New Siberian Islands

LAPTEV SEA

Os. Lyakhovskiy

Delta of the Lena

Nordvik

Kolyma

KOLYMA LOWLAND

KOLIMA MOUNTAINS

KAMCHATKA PENINSULA

Commander Is.

CENTRAL SIBERIAN PLATEAU

Indigirka

CHERSKIY RANGE

VERKHOYANSK RANGE

Lena

Magadan

Petropavlovsk-Kamchatskiy

Lower Tunguska

Yakutsk

DZUGDZHUR

SEA OF OKHOTSK

I   A

Olekminsk

ALDAN MOUNTAINS

Sakhalin

Lensk

STANOVOY RANGE

Tatarskiy Proliv

Yuzhno-Sakhalinsk

Angara

Bratsk

Krasnoyarsk

Lake Baykal

YABLONOVVY MOUNTAINS

Amur

Khabarovsk

CHINA

SIKHOTE ALIN'

Irkutsk

Lena

Yenisey MTS.

Ulan-Ude

MONGOLIA

Vladivostok

KAZAKHSTAN

N

In the Caucasus
This woman wears a traditional costume of Dagostan, a part of the Russian Federation that lies between the Caucasus mountains and the Caspian Sea. About 30 different ethnic groups live in this region.

CANADA AND GREENLAND

ARCTIC OCEAN

CANADA is the second largest country in the world and yet it is home to only 30 million people. Most Canadians live in the big cities in the south, such as Toronto, Ottawa, Montréal, and Vancouver.

The southern provinces take in the St. Lawrence River and Seaway, the Great Lakes, the prairies along the United States border, and the foggy coasts of the Atlantic and Pacific Oceans.

The severe climate makes it hard for people to live in the northern wilderness, which stretches into the **Arctic Circle**. Here, a broad belt of spruce forest gives way to bare, deep-frozen soil called tundra, and a maze of islands locked in ice.

Canada's wilderness includes rivers, lakes, coasts, and forests. It is home to polar bears and seals, caribou, moose, beavers, and loons. It also has valuable resources, providing timber, hydroelectric power, and minerals, including oil. **Canada** is a wealthy country.

The first Canadians crossed into North America from Asia long ago, when the two continents were joined by land. They were the Native American peoples and they were followed by the Inuit people of the Arctic. Today these two groups make up only four percent of the population. About 40 percent of Canadians are descended from peoples of the British Isles, especially Scots. People of French descent make up 27 percent, and there are also many people of Eastern European and Asian descent.

Canada has two official languages, French and English. In recent years many people in the French-speaking province of Québec have campaigned to become separate from the rest of Canada.

Across the Davis Strait, **Greenland** (or Kallaalit Nunaat) is a self-governing territory of Denmark. Its peoples are descended from both Inuit and Scandinavians.

Melville Island

Banks Island

BEAUFORT SEA

Prince of Wales Island

Victoria Island

ALASKA (U.S.A.)

Yukon

● Dawson

MACKENZIE MOUNTAINS

Norman Wells ●

Great Bear Lake

YUKON TERRITORY

Mackenzie

NORTHWEST TERRITORIES

▲ *Mt. Logan 19,520 ft*

● Whitehorse

R O C K Y

Liard

HORN MOUNTAINS

● Yellowknife

Dubawnt Lake

Great Slave Lake
● Fort Resolution

Fort Smith

CARIBOU MOUNTAINS

Lake Athabasca

BRITISH COLUMBIA

M O U N T A I N S

Peace

CANADA

Reindeer Lake

Churchill

● Prince Rupert

QUEEN CHARLOTTE ISLANDS

● Prince George

C O A S T   M O U N T A I N S

Fraser

● Peace River

ALBERTA

● Edmonton

N. Saskatchewan

Nelson

MANITOBA

● Red Deer

● Prince Albert

Lake Winnipeg

● Kamloops

● Calgary

Lake Winnipegosis

● Saskatoon

Vancouver Island

● Vancouver

Medicine Hat ●

S. Saskatchewan

SASKATCHEWAN

Lake Manitoba

Victoria ●

● Regina

● Winnipeg

U N I T E D   S T A T E S   O F   A M E R I C A

Wheat Harvest
Large combine harvesters cross the Canadian prairies. These are natural grasslands which are now largely given over to wheat and cattle production. They occupy parts of Manitoba, Saskatchewan, and Alberta and stretch across the border into the northern United States.

LINCOLN
SEA

Ellesmere
Island

GREENLAND

Devon Island

BAFFIN BAY

Baffin Island

Davis Strait

Denmark Strait

GREENLAND

Toronto, Ontario view over city
The CN Tower soars 1,819 feet
above Canada's largest city,
Toronto. This is a center of
business and industry built on
the shores of Lake Ontario. It is also
the capital of the vast province of
Ontario.

FOXE BASIN

LABRADOR
SEA

Southampton
Island

Hudson Strait

Coats Island

Mansel Island

Ungava
Peninsula

HUDSON BAY

Churchill

CANADA

Feuilles

Arctic travel
In the ice and snow of the
Canadian Arctic and Greenland,
traveling can be difficult.
Snowmobiles, rather like
motorcycles with skis instead of
wheels, have now mostly replaced
the traditional dogsleds.

Goose Bay

NEWFOUNDLAND

Belcher Islands

La Grande Rivière

Severn

JAMES
BAY

Akimiski
Island

OTISH
MOUNTAINS

Gander

Newfoundland

St. John's

Anticosti
Island

Gulf of St. Lawrence

Péribonca

Albany

ONTARIO

QUEBEC

St. Lawrence

PRINCE
EDWARD
ISLAND

NEW
BRUNSWICK

Charlottetown

NOVA SCOTIA

Lake Nipigon

Quebec

St. John

Fredericton

Halifax

Thunder Bay

Lake Superior

Montreal

Ottawa

ATLANTIC
OCEAN

N

Georgian Bay

Lake Huron

Toronto

Lake Ontario

Hamilton

Niagara Falls

Windsor

Lake Erie

Ice hockey
Fast and hard, ice hockey is one of
Canada's most popular spectator
sports. The game was invented in
Canada, its rules being drawn up in
Montréal in 1879. There are two
teams of six skaters. Both
Canadian and US teams compete
in the National Hockey League.

USA

THE UNITED STATES OF AMERICA

is a huge country, which crosses no fewer than eight time zones. It extends from the Pacific to the Atlantic Oceans, from Canada south to Mexico.

The modern nation was formed by colonists from Europe, who from the 1500s onward seized and settled the lands of the Native American peoples. In 1776 the British colonies in the east declared their independence, and the new country grew rapidly during the 1800s as it gained territory from France, Mexico, and Russia. Today, in addition to the small Native American population, there are Americans whose ancestors originally came from Britain, Ireland, Italy, France, Germany, the Netherlands, and Poland. There are African Americans, whose ancestors were brought to America to work as slaves. There are Armenians, Spanish, Chinese, Cubans, Vietnamese, and Koreans. All are citizens of the United States.

The nation today is a federation of 50 states, which have the power to pass many of their own laws. The federal capital is at Washington, a large city on the Potomac River, in the District of Columbia (DC). Here is the Congress, made up of a Senate and a House of Representatives, and the White House, the home of the US presidents.

The American economy is the most powerful in the world. The country is rich in minerals, including oil, coal, and iron ore. American companies produce computers and software, aircraft, cars and processed foods. There are also many large banks and finance companies. The United States leads in space exploration and technology. The films and television programmes produced in America are watched by people in many countries around the world.

FACT BOX

◆ **United States of America**
Area: 3,599,187 sq miles
Population: 267,700,000
Capital: Washington DC
Official language: English
Currency: US dollar

The woods of Vermont
Vermont is in New England and nicknamed the Green Mountain State. It is famous for its brilliant foliage in the fall.

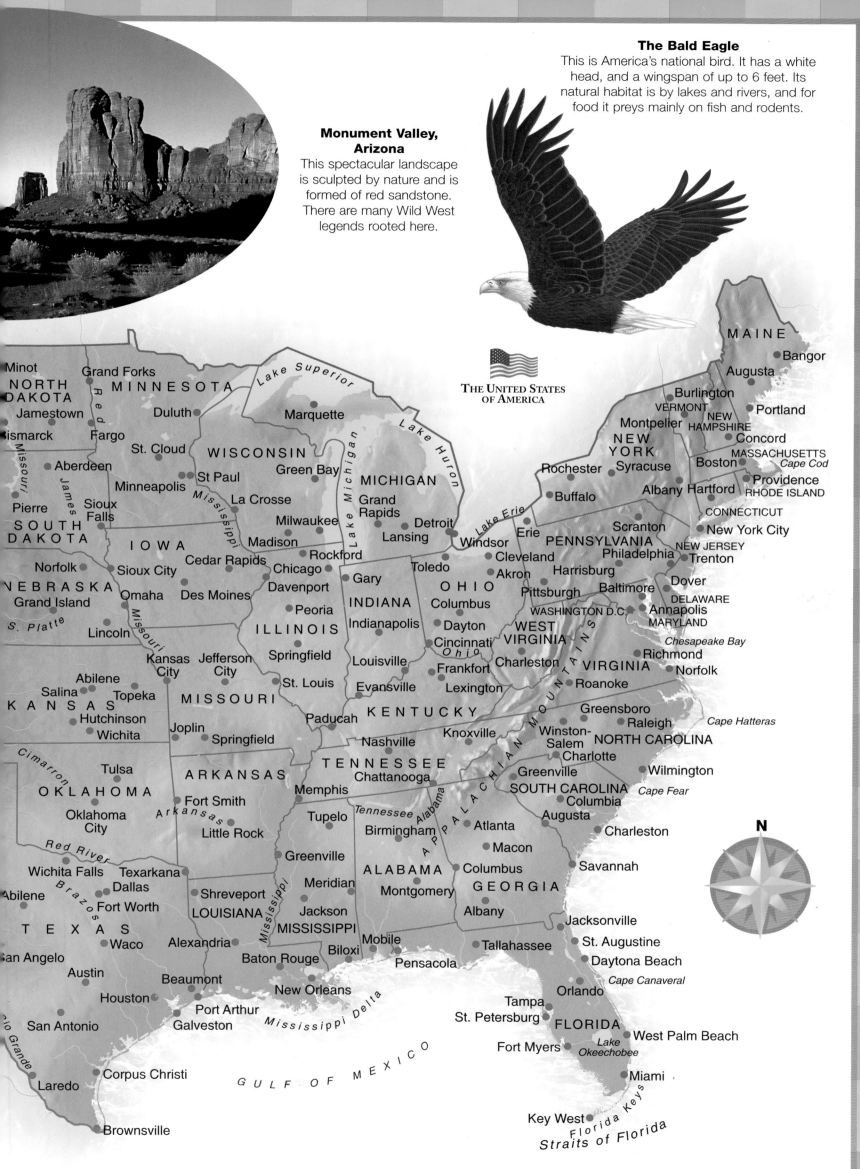

Monument Valley, Arizona
This spectacular landscape is sculpted by nature and is formed of red sandstone. There are many Wild West legends rooted here.

The Bald Eagle
This is America's national bird. It has a white head, and a wingspan of up to 6 feet. Its natural habitat is by lakes and rivers, and for food it preys mainly on fish and rodents.

THE UNITED STATES OF AMERICA

Minot
Grand Forks
NORTH DAKOTA
Jamestown
Bismarck
Fargo
Aberdeen
Pierre
SOUTH DAKOTA
Norfolk
Sioux City
NEBRASKA
Grand Island
Lincoln
Omaha
Des Moines
Salina
Abilene
Topeka
KANSAS
Hutchinson
Wichita
Kansas City
Jefferson City
MISSOURI
Joplin
Springfield
Tulsa
Cimarron
OKLAHOMA
Oklahoma City
Fort Smith
Little Rock
ARKANSAS
Red River
Wichita Falls
Texarkana
Abilene
Dallas
Fort Worth
Brazos
Shreveport
LOUISIANA
TEXAS
Waco
Alexandria
San Angelo
Austin
Beaumont
Houston
Port Arthur
Galveston
Mississippi Delta
San Antonio
Rio Grande
Laredo
Corpus Christi
Brownsville

MINNESOTA
Red
Duluth
Marquette
St. Cloud
WISCONSIN
Green Bay
St Paul
Minneapolis
La Crosse
Milwaukee
Madison
Cedar Rapids
IOWA
Rockford
Sioux Falls
Chicago
Davenport
Peoria
Gary
ILLINOIS
Springfield
St. Louis
Missouri
Lake Superior
Lake Michigan

MICHIGAN
Grand Rapids
Lansing
Detroit
Windsor
Lake Huron
Lake Erie
Erie
Cleveland
Akron
Toledo
INDIANA
Indianapolis
Dayton
Cincinnati
Louisville
Frankfort
Evansville
Lexington
Paducah
KENTUCKY
Nashville
Knoxville
TENNESSEE
Chattanooga
Memphis
Tupelo
Tennessee
Birmingham
Alabama
Meridian
ALABAMA
Columbus
Montgomery
Jackson
MISSISSIPPI
Greenville
Mississippi
Mobile
Biloxi
Pensacola
New Orleans
GULF OF MEXICO

OHIO
Columbus
Ohio
Charleston
WEST VIRGINIA
VIRGINIA
Roanoke
Greensboro
Winston-Salem
Raleigh
NORTH CAROLINA
Charlotte
Greenville
SOUTH CAROLINA
Columbia
Augusta
Atlanta
Macon
GEORGIA
Albany
Columbus
Savannah
Tallahassee
Jacksonville
St. Augustine
Daytona Beach
Cape Canaveral
Orlando
Tampa
St. Petersburg
FLORIDA
Fort Myers
Lake Okeechobee
West Palm Beach
Miami
Key West
Florida Keys
Straits of Florida

Pittsburgh
PENNSYLVANIA
Harrisburg
Philadelphia
Baltimore
WASHINGTON D.C.
Annapolis
DELAWARE
Dover
MARYLAND
Richmond
Chesapeake Bay
Norfolk
Cape Hatteras
Wilmington
Cape Fear
Charleston
APPALACHIAN MOUNTAINS

Scranton
Rochester
Syracuse
Buffalo
NEW YORK
Albany
Hartford
NEW JERSEY
Trenton
New York City
CONNECTICUT
RHODE ISLAND
Providence
Boston
MASSACHUSETTS
Cape Cod
Concord
NEW HAMPSHIRE
Montpelier
VERMONT
Burlington
Portland
MAINE
Augusta
Bangor

N

31

The northeastern states have a mild climate, although winter snowfall can be heavy and summers can be warm. Inland from the rocks and stormy Atlantic shores of the New England region are woodlands that turn to every shade of red, yellow, and gold in the autumn. Here there are wooded hills, broad rivers, and neat little towns dating back to the days of the early settlers, as well as the historic city of Boston, Massachusetts. In the far north the Great Lakes mark the border with Canada. On this border are the spectacular Niagara Falls, a major tourist attraction which also provides valuable hydroelectric power. The Appalachian mountain ranges run for 1,500 miles from north to south, through the eastern United States.

The northeastern United States include centers of industry and mining, and large cities with gleaming skyscrapers, sprawling suburbs, road, and rail networks. New York City, centered on the island of Manhattan, is the business capital of the United States and also a lively center of arts and entertainment. To many people, New York City is a symbol of America—fast-moving and energetic, a melting pot of different peoples and cultures. The northern city of Detroit is a center of the motor industry, and Chicago, on the windy shores of Lake Michigan, is another bustling city of skyscrapers, and an important center of business and manufacture.

Traveling south from the Delaware River and the great city of Philadelphia, you come to the federal District of Columbia, the site of Washington, capital city of the United States. Approaching the American South, you pass into warmer country where tobacco and cotton are grown in the red earth. The long peninsula of Florida extends southward into the Caribbean Sea, fringed by sandy islands called keys. Along the Gulf coast the climate is hot and very humid, with creeks known as bayous and tangled swamps that are home to alligators.

Hurricanes are common in late summer and autumn. New Orleans, the home of jazz, has many picturesque old buildings with wrought-iron verandas. It lies 105 miles above the mouth of the Mississippi River, which together with the mighty Missouri drains the center of the continent. Texas is a huge state bordering Mexico along the Rio Grande. Dry and dusty, it makes its living from cattle ranching and oil.

Prairies once covered the great plains of the Midwest, the home of vast herds of bison or buffalo. Today the grasslands are largely given over to farming vegetable crops and grain, or to cattle ranching. The wheat and corn produced on the Prairies have led to them being called the "breadbasket of the world."

Barren, stony "badlands" rise toward the rugged Rocky Mountain ranges, which form the backbone of the United States as they stretch from the Canadian border south to Mexico. Southward and westward again there are large areas of burning desert, salt flats, and canyons, where the rocks have been worn into fantastic shapes by wind and water. In places the Grand Canyon of Arizona is 15 miles wide and more than a mile deep, a spectacular gorge cut out by the waters of the Colorado River.

Jambalaya!
Rice, seafood, green peppers, and hot spices make up this delicious dish from New Orleans, in Louisiana. The people of this city include many of French and African descent, and this shows in its cooking.

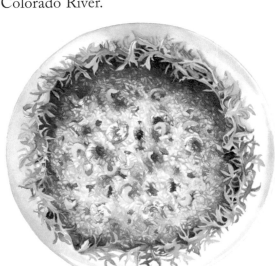

The Statue of Liberty
This huge monument, a gift from the people of France in 1886, was the first sight of America for many immigrants.

Badwater, in California's harsh Death Valley, is the lowest point in the United States, 282 feet below sea level.

The Sierra, Cascade, and Coast ranges run parallel with the beautiful Pacific coast. The warm beaches, pines, and gigantic redwood trees of California stretch northward to the ferny forests of Oregon and Washington State, which is rainy and cool. Irrigation has made it possible to farm large areas of California, which produce citrus fruits and grape vines. Major cities of the west include Los Angeles, which takes in the world-famous film studios of Hollywood, beautiful San Francisco, set on a wide bay which can be warm and sparkling blue or shrouded in cool sea-fog, and the busy northern port of Seattle.

The United States has a northern outpost in oil-rich Alaska, its largest state. Alaska was purchased from Russia in 1867. Bordered by Canada, the Alaskan wilderness stretches into the remote Arctic, a deep frozen land of mountains and tundra.

Its islands are inhabited by large grizzly bears and its waters by schools of migrating whales.

Baseball
Baseball is the the big summer game in the USA. The winners of the National and American League Championships compete in the World Series.

Mount McKinley, at 20,317 feet, is the highest point not just in the United States, but in all of North America.

Far to the west, in the Pacific Ocean, are the Hawaiian Islands, which are also part of the United States. Tourists come here to enjoy the warm climate and the surf and to see the islands' spectacular volcanoes.

The United States also governs or has special links with various other territories, such as American Samoa, the Northern Marianas, and the Midway Islands in the Pacific Ocean. Puerto Rico and the US Virgin Islands in the Caribbean are also governed by the United States.

The United States has close economic links with its neighbors, Canada and Mexico, through the North American Free Trade Agreement of 1994. It is also a member of many other international groupings, such as the the North Atlantic Treaty Organization (NATO), a military alliance linking it with Western and Central Europe.

As the world's most powerful country, the influence of the United States is to be seen in many other lands. Movies and television programs have made the American way of life influential around the world. Hamburgers and soft drinks are now bought in many other countries. American blues and jazz has influenced all kinds of popular music and American slang is used by people around the world.

Manhattan
The center of New York City is built over the island of Manhattan. Unable to build outward, architects have built upward. The skyline includes many famous skyscrapers. These twin towers belong to the World Trade Center.

Cops and crime
Policemen and detectives fight city crime. Their work has been made famous around the world by countless films and television series.

Heart of the nation
The impressive Capitol building is at the center of Washington, District of Columbia. It is used by the United States Congress and was constructed between 1851 and 1863.

Blast off!
The space shuttle leaves Earth on another mission. The United States has been a pioneer of space exploration since the 1960s.

MEXICO, CENTRAL AMERICA, & THE CARIBBEAN

Ancient stones
Many great civilizations developed in ancient times in Mexico and Central America. Statues like this, called chacmools, were used during human sacrifices.

MEXICO is a large, mountainous country with a tropical climate. It stretches southward from the Rio Grande on the United States border, and meets the Pacific Ocean in the west and the Gulf of Mexico in the east.

Mexico is a land of deserts, forests, and volcanoes, dotted with the spectacular ruins of ancient Native American civilizations, such as the Maya, Toltec, and Aztec. Mexico City, built on the site of an ancient Aztec city, is a vast, sprawling center of population.

To the south, **Central America** narrows to a thin strip of land called the isthmus of Panama. Guatemala, Belize, Honduras, El Salvador, Nicaragua, Costa Rica, and Panama are all small nations that live mostly by farming tropical crops such as bananas, coffee, and sugarcane. Many Mexicans and Central Americans are of Native American, Spanish, or mixed descent.

Birds of a feather
The quetzal is a brilliantly colored bird. It lives in rainforests from southern Mexico to Panama, where it feeds on berries and fruits.

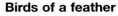

Map labels

Tijuana
Mexicali
Ensenada
Ciudad Juárez
UNITED STATES OF AMERICA
Gulf of California
Baja California
Cedros I.
Hermosillo
Chihuahua
SIERRA MADRE
Río Bravo del Norte
Rio Grande
SIERRA MADRE
Torreón
Monterrey
Culiacán
Saltillo
La Paz
Durango
San Luis Potosí
Matamoros
GULF OF MEXICO
Tampico
MEXICO
Aguascalientes
Guadalajara
León
Cape Corrientes
L. de Chapala
Mexico City
Manzanillo
Veracruz
MEXICO
Puebla
Orizaba 18,696 ft
Balsas
Coatzacoalcos
Acapulco
Oaxaca
Bay of Campeche
Campeche
Yucatán Peninsula
Terminos Lagoon
Villahermosa
Mérida
Cancún
Yucatán Channel
CUBA
Havana
CUBA
Isla de la Juventad
Cayman Islands (U.K.)
Belize City
BELIZE
Belmopan
BELIZE
GUATEMALA
HONDURAS
Tegucigalpa
Gulf of Tehuantepec
Guatemala City
San Salvador
EL SALVADOR
NICARAGUA
Managua
Lake Nicaragua
Mosquitos Gulf
San José
COSTA RICA
PACIFIC OCEAN
N
GUATEMALA
EL SALVADOR
NICARAGUA
COSTA RICA

Many people in Mexico and Central America are poor and the region has a long history of political strife and civil war.

The **Caribbean Sea** is part of the Atlantic Ocean and is dotted with beautiful islands in warm, blue seas. These were once home to Native American peoples such as the Arawaks and the Caribs, after whom the region is named. Then came European invaders, including the Spanish, Dutch, French, and British. Most of today's Caribbeans are descended from West Africans who were brought in as slaves by the early settlers. Caribbean islanders live by fishing, farming, manufacture, and tourism. Favorite sports include baseball in Cuba and cricket in Jamaica and Barbados. The region is famous for its range of popular music, from calypso to salsa, from reggae to soca.

Coconut grove
Palms line sandy beaches in the Central American republic of Costa Rica. Coconuts are common around the tropical coasts of Central America and the Caribbean.

BAHAMAS

BAHAMAS

BAHAMAS IS.

• Nassau

Andros I.

Turks & Caicos Islands (U.K.)

PUERTO RICO

Camagüey

Santiago de Cuba

HAITI

DOMINICAN REPUBLIC

San Juan

Puerto Rico (U.S.)

Santo Domingo

Port-au-Prince

GREATER ANTILLES

Kingston

JAMAICA

CARIBBEAN SEA

DOMINICAN REPUBLIC

LESSER ANTILLES

JAMAICA

HAITI

Netherlands Antilles

HONDURAS

GRENADA

PANAMA

PANAMA

Panama City

Gulf of Panama

COLOMBIA

ANTIGUA AND BARBUDA

DOMINICA

Virgin Is. (U.K. & U.S.)

ANTIGUA & BARBUDA

Montserrat (U.K.)

Guadeloupe (FR.)

DOMINICA

Martinique (FR.)

ST. LUCIA

BARBADOS

ST. VINCENT & THE GRENADINES

GRENADA

TRINIDAD & TOBAGO

ST VINCENT AND GRENADINES

TRINIDAD AND TOBAGO

ST LUCIA

BARBADOS

ST KITTS AND NEVIS

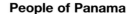

People of Panama
The Kuna are an indigenous people who live on the coasts and islands of Panama and Colombia. They mostly live by fishing and are well known for their craftwork, which includes wood carving and the making of molas, the colorful blouses being worn here.

NORTHERN ANDEAN COUNTRIES

THE ANDES MOUNTAINS extend down the whole length of South America, from north to south. They rise in Colombia, the country that borders the narrow land link with Central America, the Isthmus of Panama.

Colombia is a beautiful country with three ranges of the Andes running through it. The mountains slope east to grasslands and then to rain forest. The chief cities are on the coast, which is warm and humid, or in the cooler mountain regions. The mountains are mined for gold, emeralds, salt, and coal.

The Andes rise to 20,556 feet above sea level at Chimborazo in **Ecuador.** Bananas and sugarcane are grown here. In the cooler foothills of the Andes coffee is an important crop. To the east of the mountains are rain forests, where oil is drilled. Ecuador is the second largest oil producer in South America after Venezuela.

In the 1400s, **Peru** was the center of the mighty Inca empire, an advanced Native American civilization which produced beautiful textiles and jewelry in gold and precious stones. Ruined Inca cities such as Machu Picchu still perch high among the peaks of the Andes. Terraced hillsides allow crops such as potatoes to be grown in the mountains. Fishing is important along the foggy Pacific coast. In the far east, rivers flow through tropical forests into the river Amazon.

Lake Titicaca lies high in the Andes on the border between Peru and **Bolivia.** Bolivia is an inland country which lies across the high plateau of the Altiplano, where most Bolivians live, and stretches into hot, humid rain forest in the east. The city of La Paz is the world's highest capital city, at 12,005 feet above sea level. Bolivia produces tin, timber, rubber, and potatoes.

The lands of the northern Andes are home to many Native Americans, such as the Quechua and Aymara peoples. The whole region was ruled by Spain from the 1500s to the early 1800s, and Spanish is spoken throughout the region as well as a number of Native American languages. Although the region is rich in minerals and timber, many ordinary farmers and miners live in great poverty.

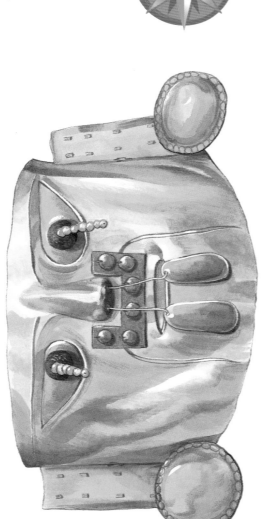

Inca crafts

This mask was made by Inca goldsmiths in Peru. The Incas came to power in the 1400s and were famous for their beautiful work with gold.

N

Point. Gallinas

Barranquilla

Cartagena ● ▲ Cristóbal Colón
18,942 ft

VENEZUELA

Meta

Guaviare

Cauca Magdalena

Medellín ● Manizales ● ■ Bogotá **COLOMBIA**
Cape Corrientes Pereira ●
PANAMA Ibagué ● ▼ Neiva
Cali ▲ Nevado del Huila
18,860 ft

Caquetá

Putumayo

Amazon

Buenaventura

Pasto ●

Point Galera

Quito ●

ECUADOR

Guayaquil ● ▲ Chimborazo
20,556 ft

Gulf of Guayaquil

Iquitos ●

Marañón

Point Aguja

Piura ●

Chiclayo ●

BRAZIL

COLOMBIA

ECUADOR

PERU

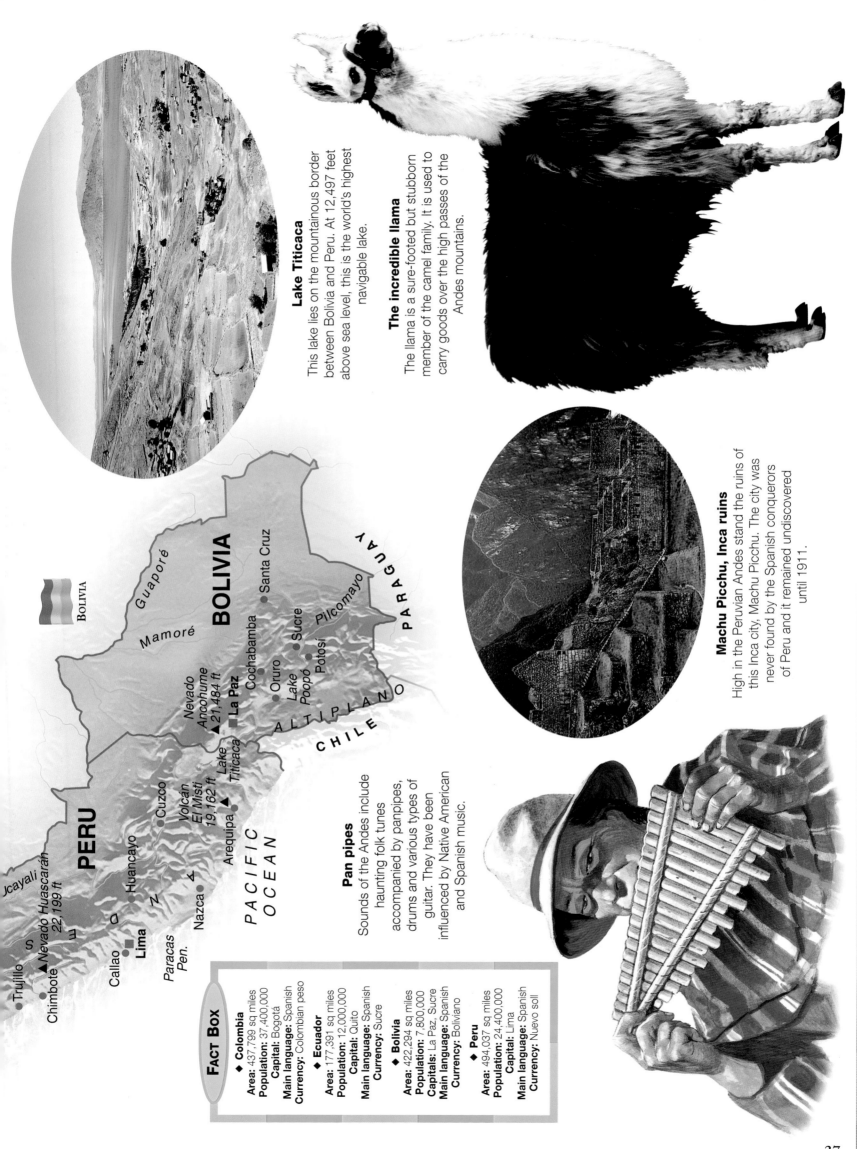

Lake Titicaca

This lake lies on the mountainous border between Bolivia and Peru. At 12,497 feet above sea level, this is the world's highest navigable lake.

The incredible llama

The llama is a sure-footed but stubborn member of the camel family. It is used to carry goods over the high passes of the Andes mountains.

Machu Picchu, Inca ruins

High in the Peruvian Andes stand the ruins of this Inca city, Machu Picchu. The city was never found by the Spanish conquerors of Peru and it remained undiscovered until 1911.

Pan pipes

Sounds of the Andes include haunting folk tunes accompanied by panpipes, drums and various types of guitar. They have been influenced by Native American and Spanish music.

BOLIVIA

PERU

BOLIVIA

CHILE

PARAGUAY

PACIFIC OCEAN

ALTIPLANO

Guaporé

Mamoré

Santa Cruz

Cochabamba

Pilcomayo

Oruro

Sucre

Potosí

Lake Poopó

Nevado Ancohume 21,484 ft

La Paz

Lake Titicaca

Volcán El Misti 19,162 ft

Arequipa

Cuzco

Nazca

Huancayo

Paracas Pen.

Lima

Callao

Chimbote

Trujillo

Nevado Huascarán 22,199 ft

Ucayali

FACT BOX

◆ **Colombia**
Area: 437,799 sq miles
Population: 37,400,000
Capital: Bogotá
Main language: Spanish
Currency: Colombian peso

◆ **Ecuador**
Area: 177,391 sq miles
Population: 12,000,000
Capital: Quito
Main language: Spanish
Currency: Sucre

◆ **Bolivia**
Area: 422,294 sq miles
Population: 7,800,000
Capitals: La Paz, Sucre
Main language: Spanish
Currency: Boliviano

◆ **Peru**
Area: 494,037 sq miles
Population: 24,400,000
Capital: Lima
Main language: Spanish
Currency: Nuevo soll

Gulf of Venezuela
Netherlands Antilles
Maracaibo
Lake Maracaibo
Caracas
Barcelona
Port of Spain
TRINIDAD & TOBAGO
Orinoco Delta

ANDES MTS.
LLANOS
Orinoco
Pico Bolivar 16,407 ft
VENEZUELA
Angel Falls
Georgetown
GUYANA
Paramaribo
SURINAME
Cayenne

GUIANA HIGHLANDS

GUYANA
SURINAME
FRENCH GUIANA

COLOMBIA

VENEZUELA

Orinoco
Branco
Pico da Neblina 9,885 ft
Negro
Japurá

FRENCH GUIANA

Macapá
Marajó Bay
Marajó I.
Belèm
São Marcos Bay
São Luis

Manaus
Amazon
Santarém
Tocantins
Teresina

S E L V A S
Madeira
Tapajós
Xingu

Juruá
Purus
Aripuanã
Araguaia
Parnaiba

Rio Branco
Jiparaná
Arinos
BRAZIL
Sobradinho Reservoir

PERU
SERRA DOS PARECIS
Guaporé

BOLIVIA

MATO GROSSO PLATEAU

Cuiabá
Brasília
Goiânia
BRAZILIAN HIGHLANDS

Uberlandia

Campo Grande
Paraná
Belo Horizonte

PARAGUAY
Campos
São Paulo
Rio de Janeiro
Cape Frio

Coffee beans
Brazil is the world's biggest producer of coffee. The crop is mostly grown in the south, on large estates and is exported worldwide.

Itaipu Res.
Itguaçu Falls
Santos
SERRA DO MAR
Curitiba

BRAZIL

ARGENTINA
Uruguay
Florianópolis

N

Santa Maria
Pôrto Alegre
Patos Lagoon

URUGUAY
Mirim Lake

Rio panorama
A huge statue of Christ stands high above the Brazilian port of Rio de Janeiro.

38

BRAZIL AND ITS NEIGHBORS

BRAZIL is South America's largest nation. It includes grasslands, fertile plateaus, and dry areas of scrub.

About a third of the country is taken up by tropical rain forests. All kinds of rare plants, parrots, snakes, and monkeys live in these dense, dripping forests, which are under threat from road builders, farmers, miners, and loggers. The forests are crossed by hundreds of rivers, which drain into the wide, muddy waters of the Amazon, one of the world's two longest rivers. The river basin of the Amazon is the world's largest, covering 2,708,100 square miles.

Most Brazilians live in the big cities of the Atlantic coast, such as Rio de Janeiro and São Paulo. The country has rich resources, but many of the population are poor people who live in shacks built on the outskirts of the city. Brasília, with its broad avenues and high-rise buildings, was specially built as the country's new capital city in the 1960s.

To the north of Brazil, on the Caribbean coast, is **Venezuela**. This land, crossed by the Orinoco River, includes rain forests, high mountains, and the tropical grassy plains of the Llanos. The beautiful Angel Falls (the world's highest at 3,211 feet) provide hydroelectric power, while Lake Maracaibo, in the northwest, is rich in oil.

The three other countries on the Caribbean coast are **Guyana**, **Suriname** and **French Guiana**. The first was once a British colony, the second was a Dutch colony and the third is still an overseas department governed by France. Most people live in the humid regions of the coast, while the rain forests and mountains of the remote south are more sparsely populated. Crops include sugarcane, coffee, rice, and bananas. An important mineral is bauxite, used in the making of aluminum.

Many different ethnic groups live in the region as a whole, including Native American peoples who have had to struggle to survive ever since Europeans invaded the region in the 1500s. The population of northern South America also includes many people of Asian, African, European, and mixed descent, with ancestors from Spain, Portugal, Italy, Germany, France, Netherlands, and Britain.

Map labels: Fortaleza, Natal, SERTÃO, Recife, São Francisco, Maceió, Salvador

FACT BOX

◆ **Brazil**
Area: 3,271,999 sq miles
Population: 160,300,000
Capital: Brasília
Main language: Portuguese
Currency: Cruzeiro real

◆ **Venezuela**
Area: 350,590 sq miles
Population: 22,600,000
Capital: Caracas
Main language: Spanish
Currency: Bolívar

◆ **Guyana**
Area: 82,634 sq miles
Population: 800,000
Capital: Georgetown
Main language: English
Currency: Guyana dollar

◆ **Surinam**
Area: 62,972 sq miles
Population: 446,000
Capital: Paramaribo
Official language: Dutch
Currency: Suriname guilder

◆ **French Guiana**
Area: 34,980 sq miles
Population: 300,000
Capital: Cayenne
Main language: French
Currency: French franc

Rain forest creatures
The vast forests that are drained by the River Amazon support all kinds of wildlife, such as this brightly colored macaw. Sadly, many species are threatened by the clearance of the forests by farmers and illegal traders in wildlife.

Fishing for a living
A fishing crew check their tackle as children play on the beach. This scene is near Salvador, capital of the tropical Bahía region in northeastern Brazil.

Yanomami hunters
About 13,000 Yanomami people live in Venezuela and another 8,000 in Brazil. They live by hunting, fishing and growing food in the rain forest.

ARGENTINA AND ITS NEIGHBORS

THE SOUTHERN PART of South America stretches from the hot and humid Gran Chaco region to the cold and stormy waters of Tierra del Fuego and Cape Horn.

The largest country of this region is **Argentina**. Its highly populated capital is Buenos Aires on the river Plate. More than eight out of every ten Argentineans are city dwellers. However it was the country's cattle-farming regions—the Pampa grasslands and the northeast—that in the last 150 years brought wealth to the country and attracted large numbers of settlers from Europe. Argentina's western borders follow the high peak of the Andes range, which reach their highest point at Cerro Aconcagua (22,826 feet above sea level). To the south are the windswept plateaus of Patagonia, largely given over to sheep farming. The port of Ushuaia is the southernmost town in the world.

Northward from Buenos Aires, across the river Plate, lies Montevideo, capital of **Uruguay**. This is another country that raises cattle and sheep, and whose rich grasslands and mild climate attracted European settlers. Neighboring **Paraguay** is far from the coast. Most of its people farm the hills and plains of the east. Few live in the hot wilderness of the Gran Chaco.

To the west of the Andes is **Chile**, which covers a long and narrow area. Here is one of the driest regions on Earth, the Atacama desert. It also includes fertile orchards and productive vineyards, the big city of Santiago and the spectacular glaciers of the southern Andes. Spanish is spoken throughout the region, and some Native American languages such as Guaraní may also be heard.

Armadillo

The head and body of the armadillo is covered by an armor of plates made of horny and bony material. These usually nocturnal animals, feed mainly on insects and rest in a burrow by day.

Paraná River, Paraguay

Separating Paraguay and Argentina the Parana River flows some 2,800 miles. The English explorer Sebastian Cabot was the first to sail up it in 1526.

BRAZIL

PARAGUAY

Concepción
Cuidad del Este
Asunción
Alto Paraná
Posadas
Salto
Paysandú
Negro
URUGUAY
La Plata
Montevideo

Verde

Pilcomayo

MESOPOTAMIA
Uruguay

Formosa
Corrientes
Resistencia

Bermejo

Paraná

PARAGUAY

Concordia

BOLIVIA

Mar Chiquito

Salado

Santiago del Estero

Córdoba

Santa Fe
Paraná
Rosario
Río Cuarto
Buenos Aires

Salta

San Miguel de Tucumán

Catamarca

La Rioja

SIERRA DE CÓRDOBA

San Luis

Arica

Calama

San Juan

Mendoza

San Juan

Iquique

ATACAMA DESERT

Antofagasta

Ojos del Salado
22,566 ft

Copiapó

Coquimbo
Pta. Lengua de Vaca

Aconcagua
22,826 ft

Valparaíso
Santiago

CHILE

Rancagua

PARAGUAY

URUGUAY

ARGENTINA

Buenos Aires by night

The Monument of the Two Congresses stands in front of the domed Palace of Congress, built in 1906. The Argentinian capital is a large, lively city.

SOUTH GEORGIA (U.K.)

N

Prickly Pear

The flesh and seeds of the peeled fruit of the prickly pear have a pleasant taste. This cactus is low-growing and has flat oval stem joints and bright yellow flowers and occurs in Central and South America.

Mountains, Southern Chile

The long, narrow country of Chile has vast differences in climate. There is hot desert in the north, Mediterranean type in the center, and cool, humid conditions in the south. Some mountains are permanently snow-capped.

FALKLAND/MALVINAS ISLANDS

Stanley

East Falkland

West Falkland

PAMPAS

ARGENTINA

Pta. de La Plata
Pta. Norte
Cape San Antonio

Mar del Plata
Cape Corrientes

Bahía Blanca

Bahía Blanca

Colorado

Viedma

San Matías Gulf

Valdés Peninsula

Rawson

Neuquén

Negro

Salado

CHILE

Talca

Chillán

Concepción
Pta. Lavapié

Temuco

Valdivia
Pta. de la Galera
Osorno

Puerto Montt

Chiloé I.

C. Quilán

LOS CHONOS
ARCHIPELAGO

Wellington I.

Penas Gulf

PACIFIC
OCEAN

REINA ADELAIDA
ARCHIPELAGO

Santa Inés I.

Limay

M
A
N
D
E
S

PATAGONIA

Chubut

Chico

Chico

Chico

Lake Buenos
Aires

Deseado

Comodoro Rivadavia

San Jorge Gulf

C. Tres Puntas

Puerto Deseado

Puerto Santa Cruz

Santo Cruz

Bahía
Grande

Río Gallegos

Strait of Magellan

Punta Arenas

Tierra
del
Fuego

C. San Diego

Ushuaia

Cape Horn

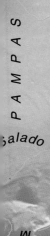

41

Turkish women
These women are from the port of Kas in southern Turkey. They are kneading dough and making pastry. Many Muslim women cover their heads with scarves or full veils.

ASIA

SOUTHWEST ASIA

SOUTHWEST ASIA IS SOMETIMES described as the Near East or the Middle East. Its peoples include Greek Cypriots, Turks, Jews, Arabs, Kurds, and Iranians.

The region has seen many political disputes and wars in recent years—between Greeks and Turks on Cyprus, between Palestinian Arabs and Jews in Israel, between Iraqi and Iranians and between Iraqi and Kuwaiti Arabs. The Kurds, whose homeland is occupied by **Iraq, Iran,** and **Turkey**, have also been at the center of conflict.

It was in Southwest Asia that the world's first civilizations grew up, between the rivers Tigris and Euphrates, more than 6,000 years ago. The region later gave birth to three world faiths —Judaism, Christianity, and Islam. In the days of the Roman empire the Jews were scattered from their homeland, and over the centuries their culture spread to Spain, Central and Eastern Europe, and the Americas. Arab armies and traders took the Islamic faith into Africa and Spain, and Arab scholars made great advances in mathematics and astronomy. From the 1500s the Turks established a great empire which stretched from Central Europe to the Indian Ocean.

Southwest Asia includes vast deserts, in the Arabian peninsula and in eastern Iran. It also takes in fertile plains, the marshes of southern Iraq, and mountain ranges of Turkey and Iran. The north of the region borders the Black Sea and the Caspian Sea, grassy steppes and the Caucasus mountains. To the east lies Afghanistan, Pakistan, and the Indian subcontinent.

The region's most valuable resource is oil, which brings wealth to the governments of the lands around the Persian Gulf. However many ordinary people of Southwest Asia remain poor, living by herding goats, sheep, or camels. In Israel and some other regions irrigation has made it possible to grow crops in harsh, dry environments. Oranges, dates, grapes, and many kinds of nuts are grown in the region.

TURKEY

SYRIA

Istanbul

Samsun

BLACK SEA

PONTIC MOUNTAINS

Gallipoli

Bursa

Sakarya

Eskisehir

Ankara

Tuz Lake

Kizil

Izmir

T U R K E Y

Kayseri

Lake Van

Konya

Gaziantep

Diyarbakir

Antalya

TAURUS MTS.

Adana

CYPRUS

Aleppo

Euphrates

Mosul

Tigris

Nicosia

S Y R I A

CYPRUS

Limassol

Tripoli

Homs

Beirut

LEBANON

SYRIAN DESERT

LEBANON

Damascus

I R A Q

Haifa

Karbala

ISRAEL

Tel Aviv

Amman

Jerusalem

ISRAEL

JORDAN

EGYPT

Elat

Al Jawf

Sakakah

A N   N A F U D

Buraydah

JORDAN

R

Medina

H I J A Z

S A U D I

Jiddah

R E D

Mecca

A S I R

Jabal Sawc 10,473 ft

S E A

Tihamah

Jaza'ir Farasan

SAUDI ARABIA

Al Hudaydah

Bab al Mandab

A summons to prayer
Mosques, like this one in Kuwait, have tall towers called minarets. From here, faithful Muslims are called to prayer. This message is often broadcast from loudspeakers. Muslims are expected to pray five times a day.

42

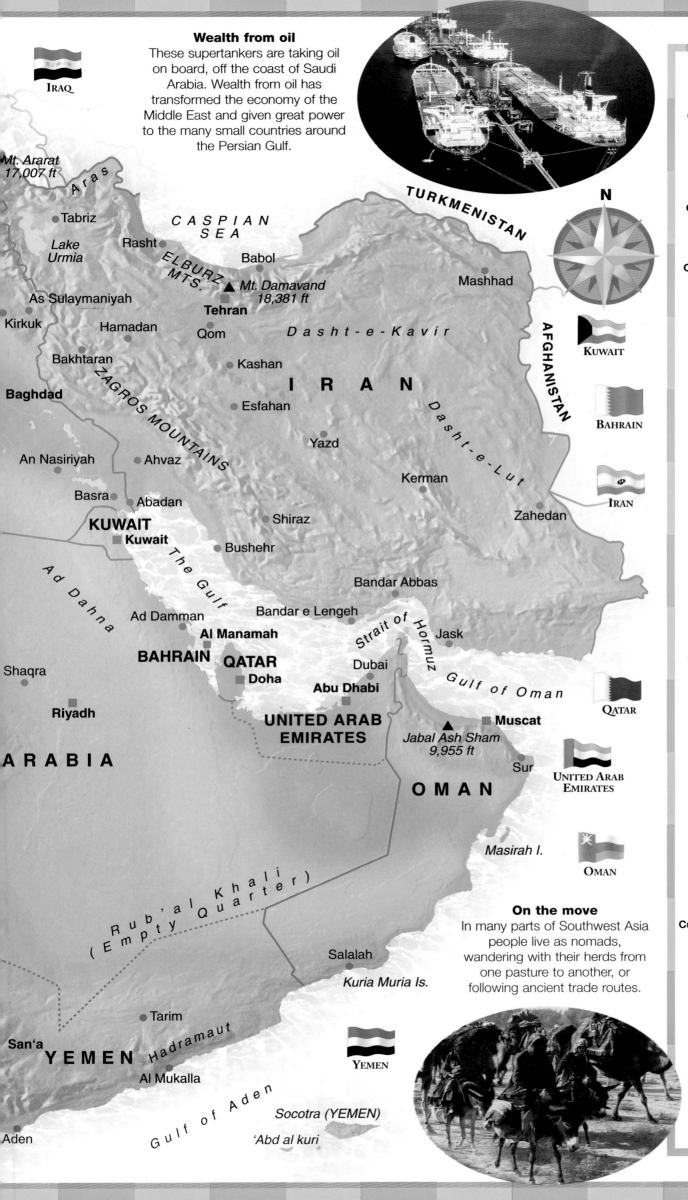

Wealth from oil
These supertankers are taking oil on board, off the coast of Saudi Arabia. Wealth from oil has transformed the economy of the Middle East and given great power to the many small countries around the Persian Gulf.

IRAQ

N

Mt. Ararat
17,007 ft
Aras
Tabriz
CASPIAN SEA
Rasht
Lake Urmia
ELBURZ MTS.
Babol
Mashhad
TURKMENISTAN
As Sulaymaniyah
▲ Mt. Damavand 18,381 ft
Tehran
Kirkuk
Hamadan
Qom
Dasht-e-Kavir
AFGHANISTAN
KUWAIT
Bakhtaran
Kashan
I R A N
Baghdad
ZAGROS MOUNTAINS
Esfahan
Dasht-e-Lut
BAHRAIN
An Nasiriyah
Ahvaz
Yazd
Basra
Abadan
Kerman
IRAN
Shiraz
Zahedan
KUWAIT
Bushehr
Kuwait
The Gulf
Bandar Abbas
Ad Dahna
Ad Damman
Bandar e Lengeh
Strait of Hormuz
Jask
Al Manamah
Gulf of Oman
BAHRAIN
QATAR
Dubai
Shaqra
Doha
Abu Dhabi
QATAR
Riyadh
UNITED ARAB EMIRATES
▲ Jabal Ash Sham 9,955 ft
■ Muscat
UNITED ARAB EMIRATES
A R A B I A
Sur
O M A N
(Rub' al Khali Empty Quarter)
Masirah I.
OMAN
On the move
In many parts of Southwest Asia people live as nomads, wandering with their herds from one pasture to another, or following ancient trade routes.
Salalah
Kuria Muria Is.
Tarim
Hadramaut
San'a
Y E M E N
YEMEN
Al Mukalla
Gulf of Aden
Socotra (YEMEN)
'Abd al kuri
Aden

FACT BOX

◆ **Cyprus**
Area: 3,556 sq miles
Population: 725,000
Capital: Nicosia
Official languages: Greek, Turkish
Currency: Cyprus pound

◆ **Lebanon**
Area: 3,998 sq miles
Population: 3,900,000
Capital: Beirut
Official language: Arabic
Currency: Lebanese pound

◆ **Israel**
Area: 7,984 sq miles
Population: 5,800,000
Capital: Jerusalem
Official languages: Hebrew, Arabic
Currency: Shekel

◆ **Jordan**
Area: 36,902 sq miles
Population: 4,400,000
Capital: Amman
Official language: Arabic
Currency: Jordanian dinar

◆ **Syria**
Area: 71,375 sq miles
Population: 15,000,000
Capital: Damascus
Official language: Arabic
Currency: Syrian pound

◆ **Turkey**
Area: 299,621 sq miles
Population: 63,700,000
Capital: Ankara
Official language: Turkish
Currency: Turkish lira

◆ **Iraq**
Area: 168,538 sq miles
Population: 21,2000,000
Capital: Baghdad
Official language: Arabic
Currency: Iraqi dinar

◆ **Iran**
Area: 633,491 sq miles
Population: 67,500,000
Capital: Tehran
Official language: Farsi
Currency: Rial

◆ **United Arab Emirates**
Area: 28,888 sq miles
Population: 2,300,000
Capital: Abu Dhabi
Official language: Arabic
Currency: Dirham

◆ **Qatar**
Area: 4,396 sq miles
Population: 600,000
Capital: Doha
Official language: Arabic
Currency: Qatari rial

◆ **Oman**
Area: 104,538 sq miles
Population: 2,300,000
Capital: Muscat
Official language: Arabic
Currency: Omani rial

◆ **Yemen**
Area: 202,952 sq miles
Population: 15,200,000
Capital: San'a
Official language: Arabic
Currencies: Yemeni riyal, dinar

◆ **Saudi Arabia**
Area: 922,906 sq miles
Population: 19,500,000
Capital: Riyadh
Official language: Arabic
Currency: Saudi riyal

◆ **Kuwait**
Area: 9,333 sq miles
Population: 1,800,000
Capital: Kuwait City
Official language: Arabic
Currency: Kuwaiti dinar

◆ **Bahrain**
Area: 254 sq miles
Population: 600,000
Capital: Manamah
Official language: Arabic
Currency: Bahraini dinar

INDIA AND ITS NEIGHBORS

SOUTHERN ASIA stretches south into the Indian Ocean, forming a landmass so large that it is sometimes called the "subcontinent." Its northern limits are marked by the Himalaya and Karakoram mountain ranges. These include many of the world's highest peaks and reach 29,021 feet above sea level at Mt. Everest, on Nepal's border with China.

The ranges pass through eastern Afghanistan, the Kashmir region on the border of India and Pakistan, India itself, and the small mountain kingdoms of **Nepal** and **Bhutan**. Melting snows flow south from the mountains to form the five great rivers of the Punjab and also the mighty Ganges, which winds across the fertile plains of northern India before crossing Bangladesh into a maze of waterways around the Bay of Bengal. This area suffers from devastating floods.

Central and southern **India** form a triangular plateau called the Deccan, fringed on the east and west by the mountainous Ghats. These slopes are forested, catching the full force of the monsoon winds which bring rains from the Indian Ocean. For most of the year India is extremely hot and dry. Indian Ocean nations include the beautiful, tropical island of **Sri Lanka** and a chain of very low coral islands, the **Maldives**.

Advanced civilizations had developed around the river Indus by about 2500 BC, and great religions grew up in India over the ages, including Hinduism, Buddhism, and Sikhism. Invaders and traders brought Islam to the region. India today is a fascinating mixture of cultures, with more than 800 different languages and dialects. There are many different customs, dress and foods. Spicy dishes from India are now popular everywhere. The Indian subcontinent has a vast population, with many hungry mouths to feed. Many people make their living by farming, growing wheat, rice, millet, sugarcane, coconut, and tea. Most industries are based in the highly populated cities of India and Pakistan.

Himalayan peaks

Breathtaking Mount Makalu, on the border between Nepal and China, rises to 27,782 feet above sea level. Eighty-eight percent of the world's mountains over 24,000 feet rise within the Himalaya-Karakoram ranges, many of them in the kingdom of Nepal.

TURKMENISTAN

TAJIKISTAN

AFGHANISTAN

Herat

Farah

Mazar-e-Sharif

Kabul

Qandahar

HINDU

DISPUTED AREA

Khyber Pass

Peshawar

Islamabad

Rawalpindi

Quetta

Sukkur

PAKISTAN

BALUCHISTAN PLATEAU

RIGESTAN DESERT

SULAIMAN RANGE

Indus

Multan

Bahawalpur

Sutlej

Faisalabad

Lahore

Amritsar

PUNJAB

Hyderabad

Karachi

Gulf of Kachch

GREAT INDIAN DESERT (THAR DESERT)

Jodhpur

Ajmer

Udaipur

Kota

Jaipur

Gwalior

Delhi

New Delhi

Agra

Yamuna

K2 28,244 ft

KARAKORAM

Srinagar

JAMMU & KASHMIR

Nanda Devi 25,640 ft

Bareilly

Lucknow

Kanpur

Allahabad

Varanasi

Ganges

Tibet (CHINA)

NEPAL

Annapurna 26,496 ft

Mt. Everest 29,021 ft

Katmandu

Ghagara

Patna

NEPAL

BHUTAN

Thimphu

BHUTAN

Brahmaputra

NAGA HILLS

Gauhati

AFGHANISTAN

PAKISTAN

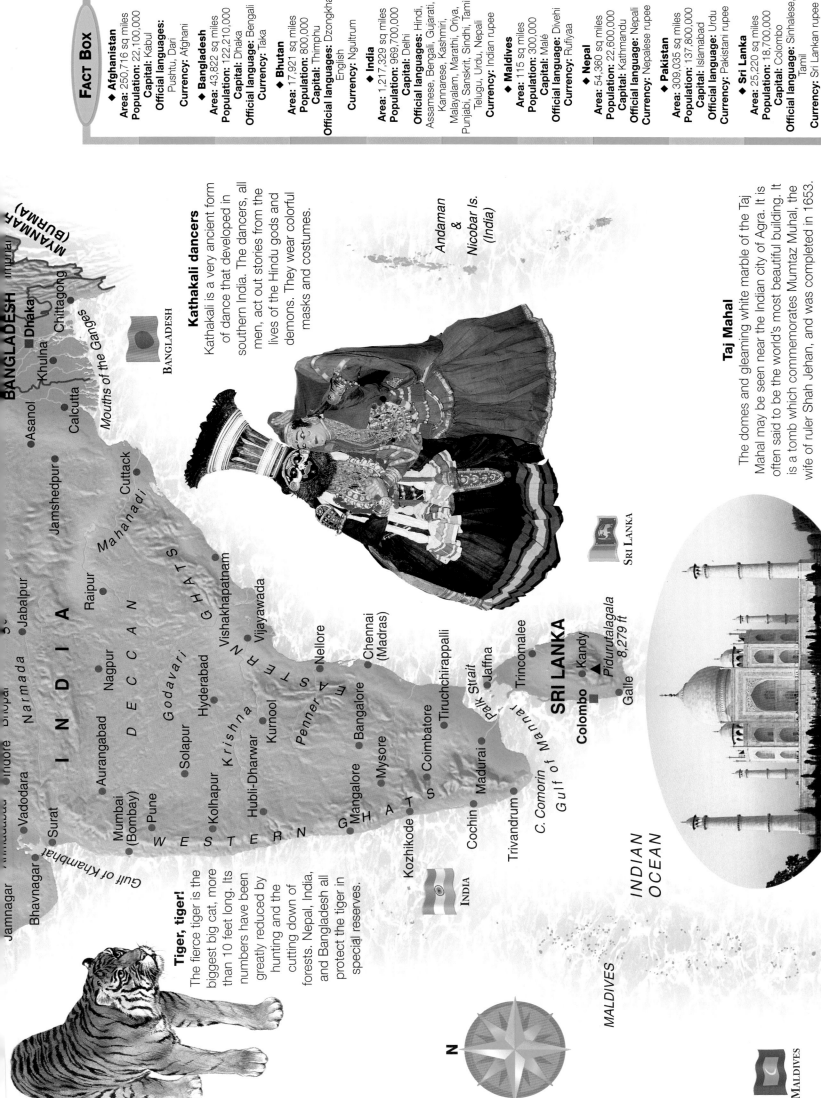

FACT BOX

◆ **Afghanistan**
Area: 250,716 sq miles
Population: 22,100,000
Capital: Kabul
Official languages: Pushtu, Dari
Currency: Afghani

◆ **Bangladesh**
Area: 43,822 sq miles
Population: 122,210,000
Capital: Dhaka
Official language: Bengali
Currency: Taka

◆ **Bhutan**
Area: 17,921 sq miles
Population: 800,000
Capital: Thimphu
Official languages: Dzongkha, English
Currency: Ngultrum

◆ **India**
Area: 1,217,329 sq miles
Population: 969,700,000
Capital: Delhi
Official languages: Hindi, Assamese, Bengali, Gujarati, Kannarese, Kashmiri, Malayalam, Marathi, Oriya, Punjabi, Sanskrit, Sindhi, Tamil, Telugu, Urdu, Nepali
Currency: Indian rupee

◆ **Maldives**
Area: 115 sq miles
Population: 300,000
Capital: Malé
Official language: Divehi
Currency: Rufiyaa

◆ **Nepal**
Area: 54,360 sq miles
Population: 22,600,000
Capital: Kathmandu
Official language: Nepali
Currency: Nepalese rupee

◆ **Pakistan**
Area: 309,035 sq miles
Population: 137,800,000
Capital: Islamabad
Official language: Urdu
Currency: Pakistani rupee

◆ **Sri Lanka**
Area: 25,220 sq miles
Population: 18,700,000
Capital: Colombo
Official language: Sinhalese, Tamil
Currency: Sri Lankan rupee

Kathakali dancers

Kathakali is a very ancient form of dance that developed in southern India. The dancers, all men, act out stories from the lives of the Hindu gods and demons. They wear colorful masks and costumes.

Taj Mahal

The domes and gleaming white marble of the Taj Mahal may be seen near the Indian city of Agra. It is often said to be the world's most beautiful building. It is a tomb which commemorates Mumtaz Muhal, the wife of ruler Shah Jehan, and was completed in 1653.

Tiger, tiger!

The fierce tiger is the biggest big cat, more than 10 feet long. Its numbers have been greatly reduced by hunting and the cutting down of forests. Nepal, India, and Bangladesh all protect the tiger in special reserves.

MYANMAR (BURMA)

BANGLADESH

Imphal

Chittagong

■ Dhaka
Khulna

Asanol
Calcutta

Mouths of the Ganges

BANGLADESH

Jamshedpur

Cuttack

Mahanadi

Raipur

Jabalpur

I N D I A

Bhopal

Indore

Narmada

Vadodara

Jamnagar
Bhavnagar

Gulf of Khambhat

Surat

Mumbai (Bombay)

Pune

Nagpur

Aurangabad

D E C C A N

Solapur

Godavari

Hyderabad

Kolhapur

Krishna

Hubli-Dharwar

Kurnool

Penner

E A S T E R N

Vishakhapatnam

Vijayawada

Nellore

Chennai (Madras)

Bangalore

Mysore

Mangalore

Coimbatore

Tiruchirappalli

Kozhikode

Cochin

Madurai

W E S T E R N G H A T S

Trivandrum

C. Comorin

Gulf of Mannar

Palk Strait

Jaffna

Trincomalee

SRI LANKA

Kandy
Colombo
▲ Pidurutalagala 8,279 ft
Galle

SRI LANKA

Andaman & Nicobar Is. (India)

INDIAN OCEAN

MALDIVES

MALDIVES

INDIA

N

45

CHINA AND ITS NEIGHBORS

CHINA is the world's third largest country in area, and has a higher population than any other. It is bordered by the world's highest mountains, by deserts, and by tropical seas.

Most people live in the big industrial cities of the south and east and on the fertile plains around two great rivers, the Huang He and the Chiang Jiang. Crops include wheat, corn, tea, sugarcane, and rice. Rice is eaten with almost every meal.

Chinese civilization dates back over thousands of years. Chinese inventions included paper and gunpowder and Chinese crafts included the making of fine porcelain and silk. Since 1949 China has been ruled by its Communist Party, but its politics are no longer really socialist. Its economy has become one of the most important in the Pacific region, and in 1997 it took back the territory of Hong Kong, an international center of business that had been a British colony. China also claims the island of **Taiwan**, which is still governed independently by Chinese nationalists who lost power in 1949.

The **Korean peninsula** saw bitter fighting between 1950 and 1953, when Korea divided into two nations, North and South. These countries remain bitter enemies today. South Korea has become an important industrial power.

Far to the north the Mongol peoples live in the independent republic of **Mongolia**. This includes the barren Gobi desert and remote grasslands.

Ulaangom
KAZAKHSTAN
HANGAY
Hovd
Fuhai
ALTAI MTS.
Karamay
Ebinur Hu
Yining
Kuytun
Dzungaria
Ürümqi
Hami
KYRGYZSTAN
TIAN SHAN
Aksu
Bosten Lake
Turfan Depression
Kashi
Yumen
TAKLIMAKAN DESERT
ALTUN SHAN
Hotan
Mt. K2
KARAKORAM
KUNLUN SHAN
PLATEAU OF TIBET
INDIA
Siling Lake
TANGGULA SHAN
Nam Lake
Tangra Lake
Lhasa
HIMALAYA
Mt. Everest 29,021 ft
Xigaze
NEPAL
BHUTAN

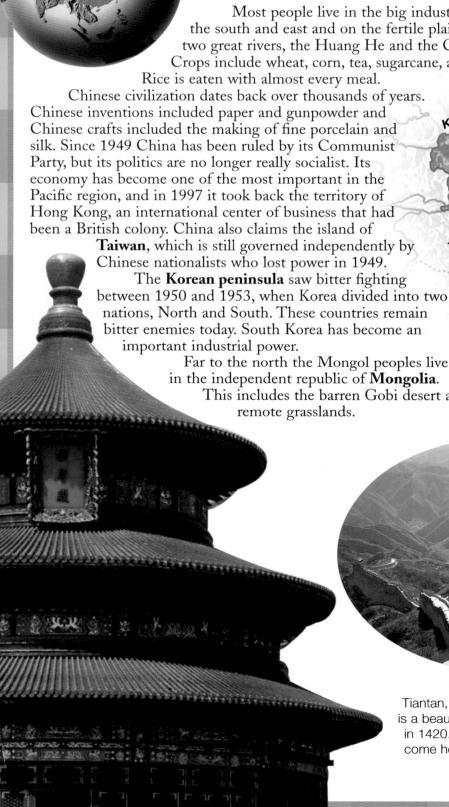

The Great Wall
A defensive wall runs across the north of China for about 3,700 miles, with many extra twists and turns. It was started in about 246 BC and added to over hundreds of years.

Temple of Heaven
Tiantan, the Temple of Heaven in Beijing, is a beautiful group of buildings first raised in 1420. The Chinese emperors used to come here to pray for a good harvest.

Xinjiang herders

These herders are from Tangbula in Xinjiang, a remote region about the size of Alaska in China's far west. Xinjiang is home to several different peoples, including Uygurs, Kazakhs, and Uzbekis.

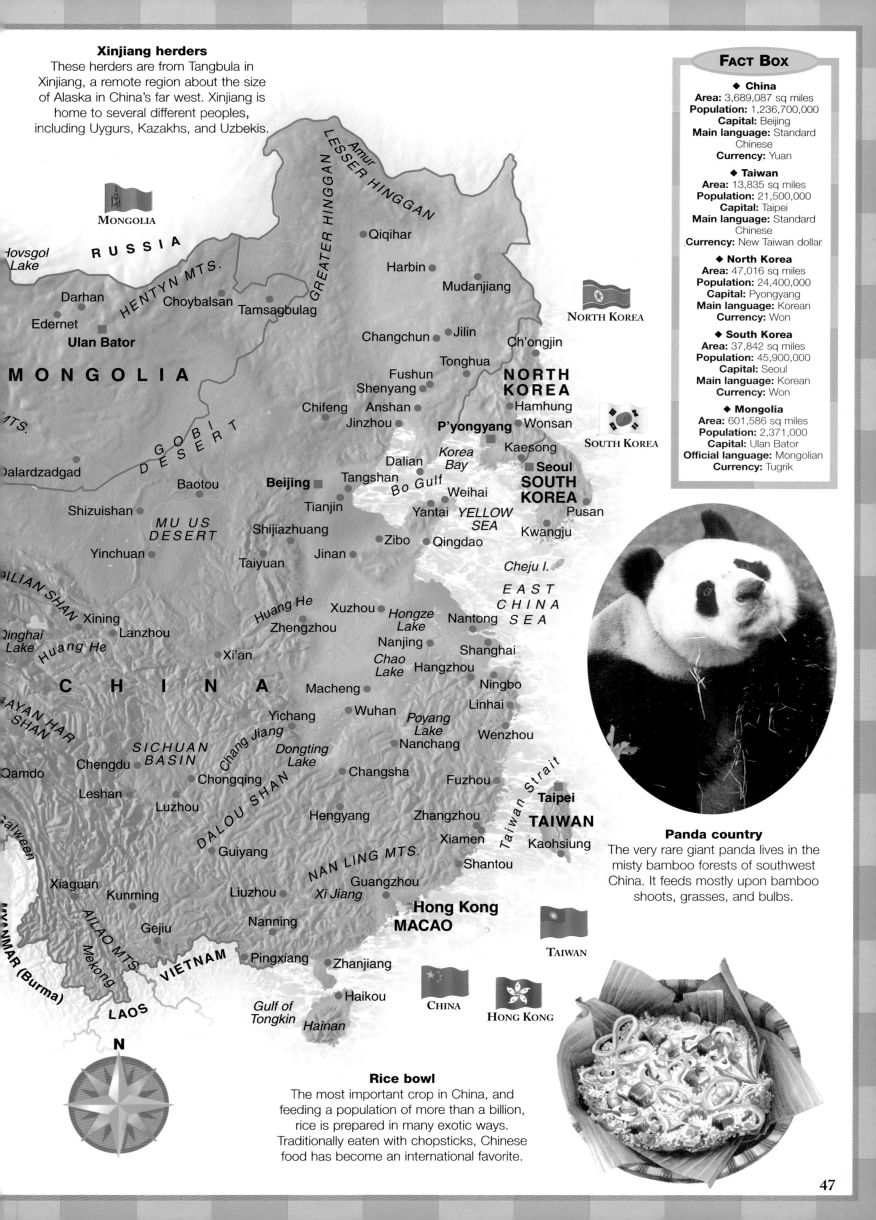

MONGOLIA

RUSSIA

Hovsgol Lake

HENTYN MTS.

Darhan
Ederbet
Ulan Bator

M O N G O L I A

Dalardzadgad

GOBI DESERT

Choybalsan
Tamsagbulag

GREATER HINGGAN

LESSER HINGGAN

Amur

Qiqihar

Harbin

Mudanjiang

Changchun • Jilin

Tonghua

Fushun
Shenyang

Chifeng   Anshan
Jinzhou

Ch'ongjin

NORTH KOREA

Hamhung
Wonsan

P'yongyang

Kaesong

NORTH KOREA

SOUTH KOREA

Baotou

Shizuishan

Yinchuan

MU US DESERT

Beijing
Tangshan
Tianjin

Dalian

Korea Bay

Bo Gulf

Weihai

Yantai

Seoul
SOUTH KOREA

Pusan

Kwangju

Shijiazhuang

Taiyuan

Zibo   Qingdao

Jinan

YELLOW SEA

Cheju I.

QILIAN SHAN

Xining
Qinghai Lake
Lanzhou

Huang He

Huang He

Xi'an

C H I N A

Xuzhou
Zhengzhou

Hongze Lake

Nantong

Nanjing

Chao Lake

Shanghai

Hangzhou

EAST CHINA SEA

BAYAN HAR SHAN

Qamdo

Chengdu

SICHUAN BASIN

Macheng

Chang Jiang

Dongting Lake

Yichang

Wuhan

Poyang Lake

Nanchang

Ningbo

Linhai

Wenzhou

Leshan
Luzhou
Chongqing

DALOU SHAN

Changsha

Fuzhou

Zhangzhou

Xiamen

Taipei

TAIWAN

Taiwan Strait

Hengyang

Guiyang

NAN LING MTS.

Liuzhou

Xi Jiang

Guangzhou

Hong Kong
MACAO

Shantou

Kaohsiung

Xiaguan

Kunming

Gejiu

AILAO MTS

Mekong

Nanning

Pingxiang

Zhanjiang

Haikou

Gulf of Tongkin

Hainan

CHINA

HONG KONG

TAIWAN

Salween

MYANMAR (Burma)

LAOS

VIETNAM

N

Panda country

The very rare giant panda lives in the misty bamboo forests of southwest China. It feeds mostly upon bamboo shoots, grasses, and bulbs.

Rice bowl

The most important crop in China, and feeding a population of more than a billion, rice is prepared in many exotic ways. Traditionally eaten with chopsticks, Chinese food has become an international favorite.

JAPAN

JAPAN is made up of more than 3,000 islands, and these stretch for about 2,000 miles from north to south on the northwest rim of the Pacific Ocean.

The chief islands are called Hokkaido, Honshu, Shikoku, and Kyushu. The islands extend from the tropical south to the chilly north, where winter snowfalls can be heavy. The region is a danger zone for earthquakes and Japan's highest mountain, Fuji, is a volcano.

The snow-covered slopes of Mount Fuji have been a favorite subject for Japanese artists over the years. Japan has a long history of excellence in art, theater, poetry, architecture, and pottery. Japanese civilization dates back more than 2,000 years. The country has been ruled by emperors and, during the Middle Ages, it was fought over by powerful warlords and bands of knights called samurai. Faiths include Buddhism and Shinto, the country's traditional religion.

Japan is very mountainous and so land that is suitable for farming is very precious. Japanese farmers grow rice, tea, and fruit and the country also has a large fishing fleet. Many meals are based on rice or fish. Japan has very few natural resources. Even so, over the last 50 years Japan has become a leading world producer of cars, televisions, and other electrical goods.

The mountains also limit the spread of housing and so Japan's cities are mostly crowded on to the strip of flat land around the coast. Tokyo has spread out to join up with neighboring cities, and now has a population of more than 25 million.

The Japanese people make up 99 percent of the country's population. The remainder includes Koreans and the Ainu of the far north, who may be descended from the first people to inhabit Japan.

Tea time

Tea is harvested on the inland slopes. The Japanese are great tea drinkers and have an ancient ceremony at which tea is specially prepared and served.

Mount Fuji

The beautiful peak of Mount Fuji, to the southwest of Tokyo, is a national symbol and, traditionally, a sacred mountain.

Sushi

Shrimp, raw fish, seaweed, pickles, and vegetables are used to make these tasty snacks. Like most Japanese dishes, they are served with rice. Japanese food is often beautifully arranged and thoughtfully served.

FACT BOX

◆ **Japan**
Area: 142,113 sq miles
Population: 126,100,000
Capital: Tokyo
Main language: Japanese
Currency: Yen

JAPAN

Kuril Is. (Russia)

La Pérouse Strait

Rebun I.
Rishiri I.
Wakkanai

Teshio

Hokkaido

Asahigawa
Asahi/Mt.
7,511 ft

Kushiro

Obihiro

Erimo Cape

Ishikari

Ishikari Bay
Otaru
Sapporo

Muroran
Uchiura Bay

Hakodate

Tsugaru Strait

Mutsa Bay
Aomori

Hirosaki

Hachinohe

SEA OF JAPAN

Morioka
Kitakam

Akita

Kamaishi

Itsukushima, Japan

Japan has many ancient Shinto shrines and Buddhist temples and many of these are set in beautiful scenery or gardens. Japan has always produced very simple and beautiful architecture and design.

Sumo wrestlers

The ancient sport of sumo is still very popular in Japan. Super heavyweight wrestlers aim to ground their opponents or force them out of the ring. There are long ceremonies before each contest.

Ride the Bullet

Japan's Bullet Train offers one of the world's most famous passenger express services. It speeds across the country, linking the capital, Tokyo, with other large cities.

A Shinto wedding

Dressed in her beautiful silk robe, or kimono, a Japanese bride sits next to her new husband, who also wears traditional costume. The wedding has been a Shinto ceremony. Shinto is an ancient Japanese faith which honors ancestors and the spirits of nature.

N

Sendai
Iwaki
Sakata
Yamagata
Abukuma
Hitachi
Niigata
Fukushima
Mito
Sado
Koriyama
Chiba
JAPAN
Nagaoka
Fukushima
Utsunomiya
Tokyo
Toyama
Ueda
Takasaki
Yokohama
Kanazawa
Matsumoto
Kofu
Kawasaki
Sagami
JAPANESE ALPS Shinano
Fukui
Takefu
Gifu
Mt. Fuji
12,385 ft
Bay
Shizuoka
O-shima
Biwa
Lake
Nagoya
Toyota
Hamamatsu
Miyake I.
Kyoto
Osaka
Matsusaka
Honshu
Kobe
Sakai
Wakayama
Hachijo I.
Matsue
Okayama
Takamatsu
Kii Channel
PACIFIC OCEAN
Oki Is.
Inland Sea
Tokushima
Shikoku
Hiroshima
Matsuyama
Kochi
Tsushima
Suo Sea
Bungo Channel
Kitakyushu
Kumamoto
Fukuoka
Omuta
Kyushu
Sasebo
Kumamoto
Miyazaki
Nagasaki
Amakusa Is.
Sendai
Tanega
Koshiki Is.
Kagoshima
Yaku

SOUTHEAST ASIA

MYANMAR is a beautiful land lying between the hill country of India and China. It is crossed by the great Irrawaddy river, which flows south into the Indian Ocean. To the southeast is **Thailand**, a country green with rice fields and teak forests. To the west lie the lands once known as Indochina—**Laos**, **Cambodia** and, on the long Mekong River, **Vietnam**.

Linked to the Asian mainland by a narrow isthmus, or strip of land, is **Malaysia**. This country also takes up the northern part of the island of **Borneo**, which it shares with the small oil-rich state of **Brunei**. Malaysia produces rubber, rice, tea, and palm oil. Kuala Lumpur is a growing center of international business with the 1,483 foot-high Petronas Towers, the world's highest building. **Singapore**, a small independent city state built on the islands across the Johor Strait, is another leader in the business world.

Indonesia makes up the world's largest island chain. It covers more than 13,600 islands, which include Sumatra, Java, southern Borneo, Bali, and Irian Jaya (the western half of New Guinea). Another large island chain, the **Philippines**, lie between the Pacific and the South China Sea.

All the islands bordering the Pacific Ocean lie in a danger zone for earthquakes and volcanoes. The region as a whole has a warm, often humid, climate, with monsoon winds bringing heavy rains. Southeast Asia's dwindling tropical forests are a last reserve for the region's rich wildlife, such as enormous butterflies and giant apes called orangutans.

Many different peoples live in Southeast Asia, including Burmese, Thais, Vietnamese, and Filippinos. There are also many people of Chinese and Indian descent. Buddhism is a major faith in the region. Most Indonesians are Muslims and the Philippines are largely Roman Catholic. During the last 50 years Southeast Asia has been torn apart by wars. The region now looks forward to a period of peace.

The face of a demon
This fierce-looking demon guards the gate of the Grand Palace in Bangkok, the capital of Thailand. Many tourists come to this kingdom, once known as Siam, to see its ancient temples and enjoy its beautiful scenery and beaches.

A dome of gold
The fantastic roofs of Shwe Dagon pagoda shimmer with gold. This holy site is in Yangon, capital city of Myanmar or Burma. The pagoda honors Gautama Buddha, the founder of the Buddhist faith.

Javanese carving
These beautiful figures, carved from stone, decorate Barobodur, on the island of Java. This 9th-century temple is the most splendid in Indonesia. Its carvings show scenes from the life of the Buddha.

PHILIPPINES
Laoag
Luzon
Mt. Pinatubo
Manila
Mindoro
PHILIPPINES
Panay
Iloilo
Tacloban
Palawan
Cebu City
Negros
Bohol
BRUNEI
SULU SEA
Mindanao
Mt. Kinabalu 13,428 ft
Zamboanga
Davao
Bandar Seri Begawan
Sandakan
Mt. Apo 9,689 ft
INDONESIA
BRUNEI
SABAH
CELEBES SEA
SARAWAK
Kapuas
Manado
MOLUCCA SEA
Halmahera
BORNEO
Balikpapan
Palu
Moluccas
Sorong
Jayapura
Barito
Sulawesi
CERAM SEA
IRIAN JAYA
Seram
NEW GUINEA
Banjarmasin
Buru
Ambon
Puncak Jaya 16,498 ft
I N D O N E S I A
PAPUA NEW GUINEA
Ujung Pandang
BANDA SEA
Aru Is.
SEA
Baubau
Digul
FLORES SEA
Wetar
Tanimbar Islands
Surabaya
Lombok
Flores
Malang
Bali
Sumbawa
Ende
Timor
Sumba
Kupang

Makassar Strait

Floating market
At a Thai market, fruit, vegetables or fish may be sold from small boats. These women traders wear broad-brimmed straw hats to protect them from the tropical sun and the heavy monsoon rains.

N

Kuala Lumpur
High-rise buildings are influenced by traditional styles in Kuala Lumpur, capital of Malaysia. "KL" is one of the most important centers of industry and business in Southeast Asia.

Komodo dragon
Meet the biggest lizard in the world, 10 feet long and weighing in at up to 300 pounds. It is found on four small islands in Indonesia, called Rintja, Flores, Padar, and Komodo.

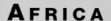

NORTH AND WEST AFRICA

THE **SAHARA** IS THE WORLD'S LARGEST DESERT, made up of more than 3.5 million square miles of baking hot sand, gravel, and rock.

Its northern fringes, occupied by **Morocco**, **Algeria**, **Tunisia,** and **Libya,** run into the milder, more fertile lands of the Mediterranean coast and the Atlas mountain ranges. They are home to Arabs and Berbers.

Deserts stretch from the Sahara eastward to **Egypt** and the Red Sea. In ancient times one of the greatest civilizations the world has seen grew up in Egypt. Then as now, the country depended on water from the world's longest

Water for sale
A Berber water seller walks the streets of Marrakech, in Morocco, offering metal cups to passers-by.

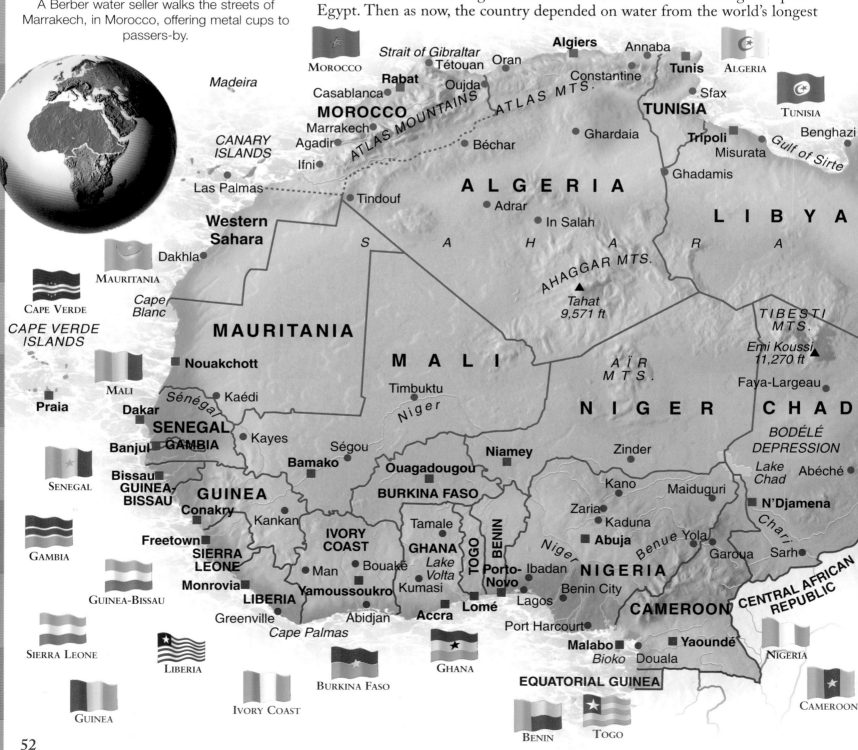

MOROCCO · Strait of Gibraltar · Oran · **Algiers** · Annaba · TUNISIA · ALGERIA · Tétouan · Constantine · **Tunis** · Madeira · **Rabat** · Oujda · Sfax · Casablanca · **MOROCCO** · **TUNISIA** · Benghazi · Marrakech · Ghardaia · **Tripoli** · Misurata · Gulf of Sirte · Agadir · ATLAS MOUNTAINS · ATLAS MTS. · Béchar · Ghadamis · CANARY ISLANDS · Ifni · **A L G E R I A** · **L I B Y A** · Las Palmas · Tindouf · Adrar · In Salah · **Western Sahara** · S · A · H · A · R · A · Dakhla · AHAGGAR MTS. · MAURITANIA · Tahat 9,571 ft · TIBESTI MTS. · Cape Blanc · CAPE VERDE · **MAURITANIA** · Emi Koussi 11,270 ft · CAPE VERDE ISLANDS · **Nouakchott** · A Ï R MTS. · Faya-Largeau · **M A L I** · **N I G E R** · **C H A D** · MALI · Sénégal · Kaédi · Timbuktu · **Praia** · Niger · BODÉLÉ DEPRESSION · **Dakar** · Zinder · Lake Chad · Abéché · **SENEGAL** · Kayes · Ségou · **Niamey** · SENEGAL · GAMBIA · **Bamako** · Kano · Maiduguri · **Banjul** · **Ouagadougou** · Zaria · **N'Djamena** · **Bissau** · **BURKINA FASO** · Kaduna · Chari · GUINEA-BISSAU · **GUINEA** · Tamale · BENIN · **Abuja** · Benue · Yola · Garoua · Sarh · GAMBIA · **Conakry** · Kankan · TOGO · Niger · **NIGERIA** · **Freetown** · IVORY COAST · **GHANA** · Ibadan · GUINEA-BISSAU · SIERRA LEONE · Man · Bouaké · Lake Volta · **Porto-Novo** · Benin City · CENTRAL AFRICAN REPUBLIC · **Monrovia** · **LIBERIA** · Kumasi · Lagos · SIERRA LEONE · **Yamoussoukro** · **Accra** · **Lomé** · **CAMEROON** · LIBERIA · Greenville · Abidjan · Port Harcourt · Cape Palmas · **Malabo** · **Yaoundé** · NIGERIA · GUINEA-BISSAU · GHANA · Bioko · Douala · **EQUATORIAL GUINEA** · BURKINA FASO · CAMEROON · GUINEA · IVORY COAST · BENIN · TOGO

river, the Nile. This flows north to the Mediterranean from the mountains of **Ethiopia** and the swamps of southern **Sudan**, Africa's largest country.

The region south of the Sahara is known as the Sahel. It includes **Senegal, Mauritania, Mali, Niger, Burkina Faso,** and **Chad**. The people include the Fulani, Kanuri and Hausa. The thin grasslands of the Sahel allow cattle herding, but droughts are common and the desert is spreading. Many people are very poor.

Thirteen nations border the great bulge of the West African coast, around the Gulf of Guinea. The coastal strip is made up of lagoons and long sandy beaches fringed with palm trees. Inland there is a belt of forest, which rises to dry, sandy plateaus and semi-desert in the far north. West African history tells of African kingdoms and empires that grew up here long ago, but also of the cruel slave trade across the Atlantic, which lasted from the 1500s to the 1800s. In the 1800s, large areas of West Africa became colonies of Britain and France. Today these lands are independent. The region has rich resources, including oil and diamonds.

Abu Simbel
When the new Aswan dam was being built in the 1960s this great temple of the ancient Egyptian ruler Rameses II had to be moved stone-by-stone.

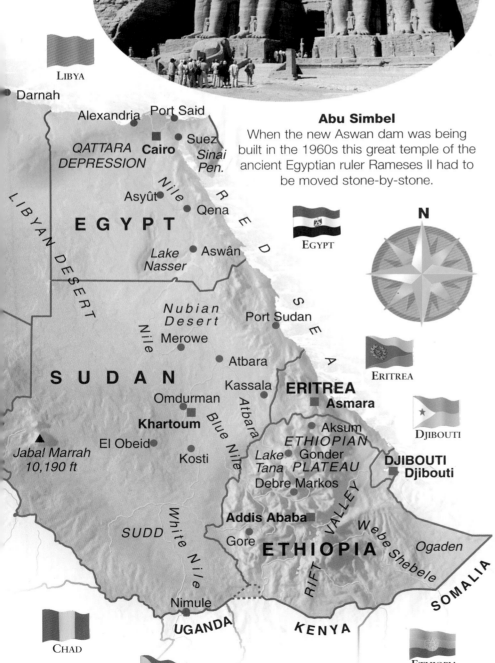

FACT BOX

◆ **Morocco**
Area: 176,336 sq miles
Population: 28,200,000
Capital: Rabat
Official language: Arabic
Currency: Dirham

◆ **Western Sahara**
Area: 96,915 sq miles
Population: 261,000 disputed territory
Official language: Arabic
Currency: Dirham

◆ **Algeria**
Area: 915,543 sq miles
Population: 29,800,000
Capital: Algiers
Official language: Arabic
Currency: Algerian dinar

◆ **Tunisia**
Area: 63,099 sq miles
Population: 9,300,000
Capital: Tunis
Official language: Arabic
Currency: Tunisian dinar

◆ **Libya**
Area: 676,367 sq miles
Population: 5,600,000
Capital: Tripoli
Official language: Arabic
Currency: Libyan dinar

◆ **Egypt**
Area: 384,496 sq miles
Population: 64,800,000
Capital: Cairo
Official language: Arabic
Currency: Egyptian pound

◆ **Sudan**
Area: 963,235 sq miles
Population: 28,129,000
Capital: Khartoum
Official language: Arabic
Currency: Sudanese pound

◆ **Eritrea**
Area: 35,211 sq miles
Population: 3,500,000
Capital: Asmara
Languages: Tigrinya, Amharic
Currency: birr

◆ **Ethiopia**
Area: 386,053 sq miles
Population: 58,700,000
Capital: Addis Ababa
Official language: Amharic
Currency: Birr

◆ **Djibouti**
Area: 8,918 sq miles
Population: 600,000
Capital: Djibouti
Languages: Arabic, French
Currency: Djibouti franc

◆ **Mauritania**
Area: 396,201 sq miles
Population: 2,400,000
Capital: Nouakchott
Languages: Arabic, French
Currency: Ouguiya

◆ **Mali**
Area: 476,710 sq miles
Population: 10,137,000
Capital: Bamako
Official language: French
Currency: Franc CFA

◆ **Burkina Faso**
Area: 105,373 sq miles
Population: 10,900,000
Capital: Ouagadougou
Official language: French
Currency: Franc CFA

◆ **Niger**
Area: 456,056 sq miles
Population: 9,800,000
Capital: Niamey
Official language: French
Currency: Franc CFA

◆ **Chad**
Area: 493,570 sq miles
Population: 7,000,000
Capital: N'Djamena
Languages: Arabic, French
Currency: Franc CFA

◆ **Cameroon**
Area: 182,782 sq miles
Population: 13,900,000
Capital: Yaoundé
Languages: English, French
Currency: Franc CFA

◆ **Equatorial Guinea**
Area: 10,782 sq miles
Population: 379,000
Capital: Malabo
Official language: Spanish
Currency: Franc CFA

◆ **São Tomé and Príncipe**
Area: 371 sq miles
Population: 124,000
Official language: São Tomé
Currency: Dobra

◆ **Nigeria**
Area: 355,128 sq miles
Population: 119,328,000
Capital: Abuja
Official language: English
Currency: Naira

◆ **Benin**
Area: 43,291 sq miles
Population: 5,900,000
Capital: Porto-Novo
Official language: French
Currency: Franc CFA

◆ **Togo**
Area: 21,828 sq miles
Population: 4,700,000
Capital: Lomé
Official language: French
Currency: Franc CFA

◆ **Ghana**
Area: 91,604 sq miles
Population: 18,100,000
Capital: Accra
Official language: English
Currency: Cedi

◆ **Ivory Coast**
Area: 129,956 sq miles
Population: 15,000,000
Capital: Abidjan
Official language: French
Currency: Franc CFA

◆ **Liberia**
Area: 43,579 sq miles
Population: 2,640,000
Capital: Monrovia
Official language: English
Currency: Liberian dollar

•**Sierra Leone**
Area: 27,802 sq miles
Population: 4,494,000
Capital: Freetown
Official language: English
Currency: Leone

◆ **Guinea**
Area: 94,518 sq miles
Population: 7,500,000
Capital: Conakry
Official language: French
Currency: Guinean franc

◆ **Guinea-Bissau**
Area: 13,886 sq miles
Population: 1,028,000
Capital: Bissau
Official language: Portuguese
Currency: Guinea-Bissau peso

◆ **Gambia**
Area: 4,109 sq miles
Population: 1,200,000
Capital: Banjul
Official language: English
Currency: Dalasi

◆ **Senegal**
Area: 75,619 sq miles
Population: 8,800,000
Capital: Dakar
Official language: French
Currency: Franc CFA

◆ **Cape Verde Islands**
Area: 1,551 sq miles
Population: 395,000
Capital: Praia
Official language: Portuguese
Currency: Cape Verde escudo

Darnah
Alexandria · Port Said · Suez
QATTARA **Cairo** Sinai Pen.
DEPRESSION
Asyût · Qena
E G Y P T
Lake Nasser · Aswân

EGYPT

LIBYAN DESERT
Nubian Desert
Port Sudan
Merowe
Atbara
S U D A N
Kassala
Omdurman
Khartoum
Jabal Marrah 10,190 ft
El Obeid
Kosti
SUDD
White Nile
Nimule
UGANDA
KENYA

ERITREA
Asmara
Aksum
ETHIOPIAN
Lake Gonder
Tana PLATEAU
Debre Markos
Addis Ababa
Gore **ETHIOPIA**
Webe Shebele
Ogaden
RIFT VALLEY
SOMALIA
Blue Nile
Atbara

DJIBOUTI
Djibouti

N

CENTRAL, EASTERN, & SOUTHERN AFRICA

CENTRAL AFRICA is dominated by the river Congo, which flows through hot and humid rainforest to the Atlantic Ocean. The great river winds through the **Democratic Republic of the Congo**, and the network of waterways that drain into it provide transportation routes for riverboats and canoes.

A long crack in the Earth's crust, the Great Rift Valley, runs all the way down **East Africa**. Its route is marked by volcanoes and lakes. Some East African mountains remain snow-capped all year round, even though they are on the Equator. The highest of these is Kilimanjaro, at 19,516 feet. It looks out over savanna, grasslands dotted with trees. Huge herds of wildlife roam these plains. Zebra, giraffe, elephants, and lions are protected within national parks. The Indian Ocean coast includes white beaches and coral islands. Mombasa, Dar-es-Salaam, and Maputo are major ports.

In southern Africa the Drakensberg mountains descend to grassland known as veld. There are harsh deserts too, the Kalahari and the Namib. The **Republic of South Africa** is one of the most powerful countries in Africa. It has ports at Durban and Capetown.

Central and southern Africa are rich in mineral resources, including gold, diamonds, and copper. Eastern and southern Africa are important farming regions, raising cattle and producing coffee, vegetables, tropical fruits, tobacco, and grape vines.

African kingdoms flourished in the Congo region in the Middle Ages and the stone ruins of Great Zimbabwe recall gold traders of long ago. Today the region is home to hundreds of African peoples with many different languages and cultures.

Magnificent Masai
This young Masai girl wears her traditional beaded necklace and headdress. These noble, nomadic people herd cattle and live mainly in Kenya and Tanzania.

La Digue, Seychelles
More than 100 islands make up the Seychelles. La Digue is only 6 miles in area, but the third most populated.

Cape Caseyr

Berbera

SOMALIA

KENYA

UGANDA

ETHIOPIA

Lake Turkana

KENYA

Kisumu   Mt. Kenya
▲ 17,053 ft

Mogadishu

Lake Victoria   Nairobi

Kismayu

Mwanza

Kilimanjaro
19,336 ft

Mombasa

Dodoma

Zanzibar
Dar-es-Salaam

TANZANIA

Lake Nyasa

MALAWI

Lilongwe

Blantyre

MOZAMBIQUE

Beira

MOZAMBIQUE

ZIMBABWE

Tana

Juba

Rufiji

BURUNDI

MALAWI

SOMALIA

INDIAN OCEAN

N

SEYCHELLES

Aldabra Is.

SEYCHELLES

COMOROS   C. d'Ambre

Antisiranana

MADAGASCAR

C. Delgado

Moçambique

Mozambique Channel

Mahajanga

Toamasina

MAURITIUS

Antananarivo

MADAGASCAR

MAURITIUS

Réunion
(France)

Fianarantsoa

C. Ste. Marie

Sting in the tail
Scorpions always look threatening. The curled-forward tail contains a sting which can be deadly. They eat insects and other animals which they catch with their claws. They are most common in desert areas.

FACT BOX

◆ **Central African Republic**
Area: 246,240 sq miles
Population: 3,300,000
Capital: Bangui
Main language: French
Currency: Franc CFA

◆ **Gabon**
Area: 102,890 sq miles
Population: 1,200,000
Capital: Libreville
Main language: French
Currency: Franc CFA

◆ **Republic of Congo**
Area: 131,465 sq miles
Population: 2,500,000
Capital: Brazzaville
Main language: French
Currency: Franc CFA

◆ **Democratic Republic of Congo (Zaïre)**
Area: 901,576 sq miles
Population: 46,500,000
Capital: Kinshasa
Main language: French
Currency: Zaïre

◆ **Rwanda**
Area: 10,121 sq miles
Population: 6,900,000
Capital: Kigali
Main languages: Kinyarwanda, French
Currency: Rwanda franc

◆ **Burundi**
Area: 10,700 sq miles
Population: 5,900,000
Capital: Bujumbura
Main languages: Kirundi, French
Currency: Burundi franc

◆ **Uganda**
Area: 90,941 sq miles
Population: 22,000,000
Capital: Kampala
Main language: English
Currency: Uganda shilling

◆ **Kenya**
Area: 223,969 sq miles
Population: 28,200,000
Capital: Nairobi
Main languages: Swahili, English
Currency: Kenya shilling

◆ **Somalia**
Area: 242,172 sq miles
Population: 9,500,000
Capital: Mogadishu
Main languages: Somali, Arabic
Currency: Somali shilling

◆ **Tanzania**
Area: 361,245 sq miles
Population: 29,100,000
Capital: Dodoma
Main languages: Swahili, English
Currency: Tanzanian shilling

◆ **Seychelles**
Area: 155 sq miles
Population: 100,000
Capital: Victoria
Official languages: English, French, Creole
Currency: Seychelles rupee

◆ **Comoros**
Area: 715 sq miles
Population: 600,000
Capital: Moroni
Official languages: Arabic, French
Currency: Comorian franc

◆ **Mauritius**
Area: 717 sq miles
Population: 1,100,000
Capital: Port Louis
Official language: English

◆ **Madagascar**
Area: 228,403 sq miles
Population: 15,200,000
Capital: Antananarivo
Official languages: Malagasy, French
Currency: Malagasy franc

◆ **Mozambique**
Area: 301 660 sq miles
Population: 16,500,000
Capital: Maputo
Official language: Portuguese
Currency: Metical

◆ **Malawi**
Area: 36,164 sq miles
Population: 9,500,000
Capital: Lilongwe
Official language: Chichewa, English
Currency: Kwacha

◆ **Zambia**
Area: 289,305 sq miles
Population: 9,200,000
Capital: Lusaka
Official language: English
Currency: Kwacha

◆ **Zimbabwe**
Area: 150,035 sq miles
Population: 11,500,000
Capital: Harare
Official language: English
Currency: Zimbabwe dollar

◆ **Botswana**
Area: 221,030 sq miles
Population: 1,500,000
Capital: Gaborone
Official language: English
Currency: Pula

◆ **Lesotho**
Area: 11,665 sq miles
Population: 2,100,000
Capital: Maseru
Official languages: Sesotho, English
Currency: Loti

◆ **Swaziland**
Area: 6,675 sq miles
Population: 1,000,000
Capital: Mbabane
Official languages: Swazi, English
Currency: Lilangeni

◆ **South Africa**
Area: 469,293 sq miles
Population: 44,500,000
Capitals: Pretoria, Cape Town
Official languages: Afrikaans, English, Ndebele, Sesotho, Swazi, Tsonga, Tswana, Venda, Xhodsa, Zulu
Currency: Rand

◆ **Namibia**
Area: 316,859 sq miles
Population: 1,600,000
Capital: Windhoek
Official language: English
Currency: Namibian dollar

◆ **Angola**
Area: 479,231 sq miles
Population: 11,500,000
Capital: Luanda
Official language: Portuguese
Currency: Kwanza

AUSTRALIA

THIS COUNTRY is the size of a continent, a huge mass of land surrounded by ocean. The heart of **Australia** is a vast expanse of baking desert, salt pans, shimmering plains, and dry scrubland. Ancient, rounded rocks glow in the morning and evening sun.

These barren lands are fringed by grasslands, tropical forests, creeks, and fertile farmland. In the far east is the Great Dividing Range, which rises to the high peaks of the Australian Alps. The southeast is crossed by the Murray and Darling rivers. The Great Barrier Reef, the world's largest coral reef, stretches for more than 1,200 miles off the eastern coast, while the island of Tasmania lies to the south across the Bass Strait.

Most Australians don't live in the "Outback," the dusty back country with its huge sheep and cattle stations and its mines. They live in big coastal cities such as Brisbane, Sydney, Adelaide, and Perth. There they enjoy a high standard of living, an outdoor lifestyle, sunshine, and surfing.

To the many people who in recent years have come from Europe and Asia to settle in Australia, this seems like a new country. However it is really a very ancient land, cut off from other parts of the world so long that it has many animals seen nowhere else on Earth, such as kangaroos, echidnas, and platypuses.

Australia has probably been home to Aboriginal peoples for more than 50,000 years. European settlement began in 1788, when the British founded a prison colony at Botany Bay, near today's city of Sydney. Many Australians still like to keep in touch with British relatives and traditions, but the modern country follows its own path as one of the great economic powers of the Pacific region.

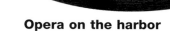

Opera on the harbor

Sydney's most famous landmark is its Opera House, built between 1959 and 1973. It rises from the blue waters of the harbor like a great sailing ship. Sydney, the capital of New South Wales, is Australia's biggest city with a population of about 3,700,000.

Christmas beetles

Australia and its surrounding islands are populated by many weird and wonderful insects and beetles. These beetles are from Christmas Island.

Bonaparte Archipelago

Broome

Fitzroy

Eighty Mile Beach

Port Hedland

De Grey

Barrow I.

Fortescue

Ashburton

Mt. Bruce

GIBSON DESERT

Lake Macleod

Carnarvon

Murchison

Dirk Hartog I.

WESTERN AUSTRALIA

Geraldton

Laverton

Kalgoorlie-Boulder

Perth

Fremantle

Bunbury

C. Naturaliste

Archipelago of the Recherche

C. Leeuwin

Albany

Aboriginal art

An Aboriginal artist from Groote Eylandt, an island in the Gulf of Carpentaria, completes a painting on bark. Paintings by Australia's Aborigines are admired around the world. They often recall the ancient myths and legends of their people, with bold, swirling patterns or pictures of animals.

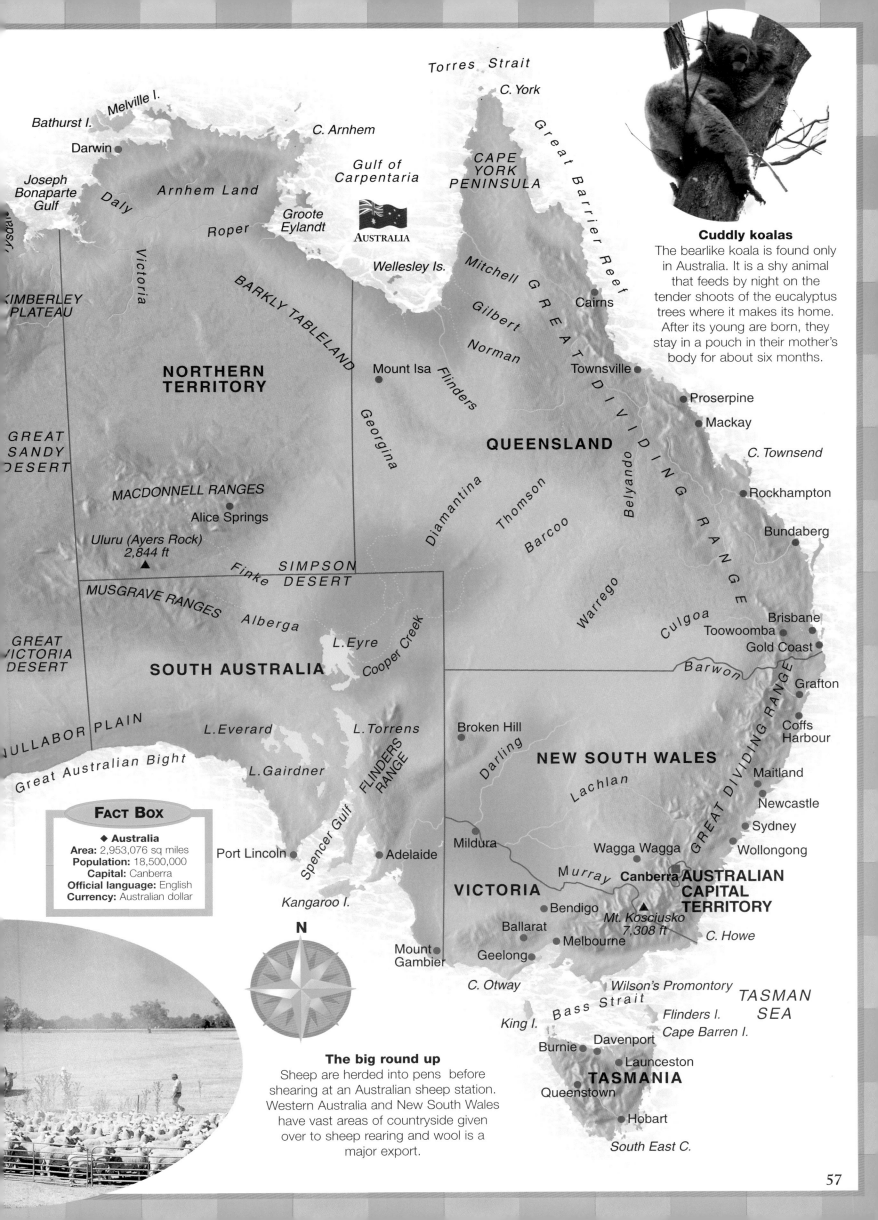

Torres Strait
C. York
Melville I.
Bathurst I.
Darwin
C. Arnhem
Gulf of Carpentaria
CAPE YORK PENINSULA
Great Barrier Reef
Joseph Bonaparte Gulf
Daly
Arnhem Land
Groote Eylandt
Roper
Victoria
AUSTRALIA
Wellesley Is.
Mitchell
KIMBERLEY PLATEAU
BARKLY TABLELAND
Gilbert
Norman
Cairns
GREAT DIVIDING RANGE

Cuddly koalas
The bearlike koala is found only in Australia. It is a shy animal that feeds by night on the tender shoots of the eucalyptus trees where it makes its home. After its young are born, they stay in a pouch in their mother's body for about six months.

NORTHERN TERRITORY
Mount Isa
Flinders
Townsville
Proserpine
Mackay

GREAT SANDY DESERT
Georgina
QUEENSLAND
C. Townsend
Rockhampton

MACDONNELL RANGES
Alice Springs
Diamantina
Thomson
Barcoo
Belyando
Bundaberg

Uluru (Ayers Rock) 2,844 ft
Finke
SIMPSON DESERT
MUSGRAVE RANGES
Alberga
Warrego

GREAT VICTORIA DESERT
L. Eyre
Cooper Creek
Culgoa
Brisbane
Toowoomba
Gold Coast
Barwon

SOUTH AUSTRALIA
NULLABOR PLAIN
L. Everard
L. Torrens
L. Gairdner
FLINDERS RANGE
Broken Hill
Darling
NEW SOUTH WALES
Lachlan
Grafton
Coffs Harbour
Maitland
Newcastle
Sydney
Wollongong

Great Australian Bight

FACT BOX

◆ **Australia**
Area: 2,953,076 sq miles
Population: 18,500,000
Capital: Canberra
Official language: English
Currency: Australian dollar

Port Lincoln
Spencer Gulf
Adelaide
Mildura
Wagga Wagga
Canberra
AUSTRALIAN CAPITAL TERRITORY

Kangaroo I.
VICTORIA
Bendigo
Mt. Kosciusko 7,308 ft
C. Howe

N

Mount Gambier
Ballarat
Melbourne
Geelong
Murray
Mt. Gambier

C. Otway
Wilson's Promontory
TASMAN SEA
King I.
Bass Strait
Flinders I.
Cape Barren I.

The big round up
Sheep are herded into pens before shearing at an Australian sheep station. Western Australia and New South Wales have vast areas of countryside given over to sheep rearing and wool is a major export.

Burnie
Davenport
Launceston
TASMANIA
Queenstown
Hobart
South East C.

NEW ZEALAND AND THE PACIFIC

NEW ZEALAND LIES in the Pacific Ocean, about 1,000 miles to the east of Australia. It has a moist, mild climate and many unusual plants, birds, and animals may be found there.

Most of its people live on North Island and South Island. These beautiful islands, divided by the Cook Strait, are the largest of several which are included within the country. North Island has volcanoes, hot springs, and gushing geysers. South Island is dominated by the peaks and glaciers of the Southern Alps. It also has deep sea inlets called fiords and rolling grassy plains. New Zealand, with its sheep, cattle, and fruit farms, has one of the most important economies in the Pacific region.

Papua New Guinea is another island nation, bordering Indonesian territory on the island of New Guinea. It also includes several chains of smaller islands. Many of its mountain regions, blanketed in tropical forests, were only opened up to the outside world in the 20th century. The country is rich in mineral resources and its fertile soils produce coffee, tea, and rubber.

Strung out eastward, across the lonely Pacific Ocean are many scattered island chains and reefs. Small coral islands surround peaceful blue lagoons ringed with palm trees. The islanders may make their living by fishing, growing coconuts, mining, or tourism. Many of the island groups have banded together to form independent nation states.

Peoples of the Pacific are of varied descent. Some are the descendants of European settlers—for example the British in New Zealand, or the French on New Caledonia or Tahiti. Fiji has a large population of Indian descent. The original peoples of the Pacific fall into three main groups. Melanesians, such as the Solomon Islanders, live in the western Pacific, while Micronesians live in the Caroline and Marshall Islands. The Polynesian peoples, brilliant seafarers, colonized vast areas of the ocean, from New Zealand to the Hawaiian Islands. The Maoris, who make up nine percent of New Zealand's population, are a Polynesian people who have kept and valued many of their ancient traditions.

SEA OF JAPAN

Yellow Sea

East China Sea

MICRONESIA

SOLOMON ISLANDS

Northern Mariana Islands (USA)

SOUTH CHINA SEA

Philippine Sea

Guam (USA)

Federated States of Micronesia

Celebes Sea

Palau

Papua New Guinea

Irian Jaya (Indonesia)

Solomon Islands

Arafura Sea

Port Moresby

Coral Sea

AUSTRALIA

TASMAN SEA

New Guinea finery
Feathers and paint are worn by many young warriors at tribal gatherings and feasts in remote areas of Papua New Guinea. The country has a rich culture with more than 860 different languages.

Kiwi fruit
When farmers decided to grow this fruit in New Zealand, they decided to give it a local name to help sales. The kiwi is the national bird, and a nickname for a New Zealander.

BERING SEA

PAPUA NEW
GUINEA

PALAU

_N O R T H
P A C I F I C
O C E A N_

Midway Island
(USA)

Wake Island
(USA)

VANUATU

Marshall Island

MARSHALL
ISLANDS

Hawaii (USA)

KIRIBATI

NAURU

Nauru

Kiribati

Tuvalu

TUVALU

SAMOA

Samoa

American
Samoa

_S O U T H
P A C I F I C
O C E A N_

Galapagos
(Ecuador)

Vanuatu

Fiji

Tonga

New Caledonia
(France)

Cook Islands
(New Zealand)

French
Polynesia

Pitcairn Island
(UK)

Easter Island
(Chile)

FIJI

TONGA

NEW ZEALAND

**NEW
ZEALAND**

Easter Island
Hundreds of huge, mysterious stone heads tower above the hills of Easter Island, in the eastern Pacific. They were erected by Polynesians about 1,000 years ago. Today Easter Island is governed by Chile.

Gusher!
Steam bursts from volcanic rocks near Rotorua on North Island. New Zealand's geysers and hot springs are not just a tourist attraction. They are used to generate electricity.

◆ **Papua New Guinea**
Area: 177,916 sq miles
Population: 4,400,000
Capital: Port Moresby
Official language: English
Currency: Kina

◆ **New Zealand**
Area: 101,924 sq miles
Population: 3,600,000
Capital: Auckland
Official language: English
Currency: New Zealand dollar

◆ **Palau**
Area: 188 sq miles
Population: 16,000
Capital: Koror
Official languages: Palauan,
English
Currency: US dollar

◆ **Marshall Islands**
Area: 70 sq miles
Population: 52,000
Capital: Majuro
Official language: Marshallese,
English
Currency: US dollar

◆ **Solomon Islands**
Area: 11,451 sq miles
Population: 354,000
Capital: Honiara
Official language: English
Currency: Solomon Islands
dollar

◆ **Tuvalu**
Area: 10 sq miles
Population: 13,000
Capital: Funafuti
Official languages: Tuvaluan,
English
Currency: Australian dollar

◆ **Kiribati**
Area: 263 sq miles
Population: 75,000
Capital: Bairiki
Official language: English
Currency: Australian dollar

◆ **Nauru**
Area: 8 sq miles
Population: 10,000
Capital: Yaren
Official language: Nauruan
Currency: Australian dollar

◆ **Fiji**
Area: 7,046 sq miles
Population: 758,000
Capital: Suva
Official language: English
Currency: Fiji dollar

◆ **Tonga**
Area: 269 sq miles
Population: 103,000
Capital: Nukualofa
Official languages: Tongan,
English
Currency: Pa'anga

◆ **Vanuatu**
Area: 5,676 sq miles
Population: 156,000
Capital: Porta-Vila
Official languages: Bislama,
English, French
Currency: Vatu

◆ **Western Samoa**
Area: 1,092 sq miles
Population: 170,000
Capital: Apia
Official languages: Samoan,
English
Currency: Tala

◆ **Federated States of
Micronesia**
Area: 270 sq miles
Population: 114,000
Capital: Kolonia
Official language: English
Currency: US dollar

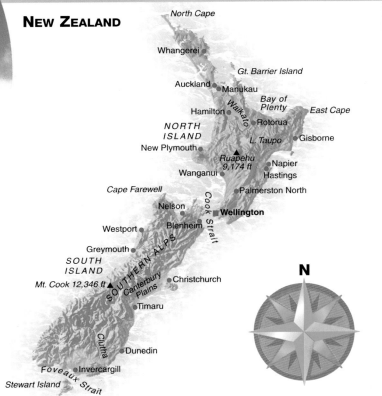

NEW ZEALAND

North Cape

Whangerei

Gt. Barrier Island

Auckland
Manukau

Bay of
Plenty

East Cape

Hamilton

Waikato

_NORTH
ISLAND_

Rotorua

L. Taupo

Gisborne

New Plymouth

▲ _Ruapehu_
9,174 ft

Napier

Wanganui

Hastings

Cape Farewell

Palmerston North

Nelson

Cook Strait

Wellington

Westport

Blenheim

Greymouth

SOUTHERN ALPS

Christchurch

_SOUTH
ISLAND_

_Canterbury
Plains_

Mt. Cook 12,346 ft ▲

Timaru

Clutha

N

Dunedin

Invercargill

Foveaux Strait

Stewart Island

POLAR LANDS

THE NORTHERNMOST PART of our globe is called the Arctic. Within this bitterly cold region lie the northern borders of Alaska (part of the United States), Canada, Greenland (a self-governing territory of Denmark), Norway, Sweden, Finland, and Russia.

Living in the Arctic
The Inuit peoples of northern Canada and Greenland have always lived by hunting and fishing and are experts at surviving in the harsh climate.

However, most of the area is covered by the Arctic Ocean, much of which is frozen solid all year round. At the center of this great cap of ice is the North Pole. The **Arctic** supports a surprisingly wide selection of wildlife, including seals, walruses and polar bears. Peoples who have learned to live permanently in the far north include the Aleuts, the Inuit, the Saami, the Yakuts, and the Chukchi. They have been joined in recent years by workers from the oil industry.

The only people to be found in **Antarctica**, at the other end of the globe, are scientists studying the weather and rocks of the coldest and windiest continent on Earth. The only other living things to survive here are the penguins which breed around the coast and the whales, birds, and fishes of the Southern Ocean. The land mass is ringed by a shelf of ice, some of which breaks away to form massive icebergs in the spring. Inland there are mountain ranges and icy plains. The Antarctic winter takes place during the Arctic summer, and the Antarctic summer during the Arctic winter.

Various countries claim territory in Antarctica, and the continent is rich in minerals and fishing. However many scientists argue that this land should never be opened up to mining and industry, but left as the planet's last true wilderness.

Yukon · Bering Strait · ALASKA (USA) · CHUKCHI SEA · Ambarchik · Kolyma · Indigirka · RUSSIA · Barrow · Pt. Barrow · EAST SIBERIAN SEA · Mackenzie · BEAUFORT SEA · New Siberian Islands · Lena · C.Bathurst · CANADA · Banks Island · McClure Strait · ARCTIC OCEAN · LAPTEV SEA · Victoria Island · Nordvik · Queen Elizabeth Islands · North Magnetic Pole · Severnaya Zemlya · Yenisei · ★ North Pole · Dikson · Ellesmere Island · LINCOLN SEA · Franz Josef Land · Foxe Basin · Baffin Island · Baffin Bay · Novaya Zemlya · KARA SEA · Ob' · Davis Strait · GREENLAND (DENMARK) · Svalbard (Norway) · BARENTS SEA · Pechora · GREENLAND SEA · North Cape · Godthåb · Murmansk · Denmark Strait · NORWEGIAN SEA · Archangel · ICELAND · Reykjavik

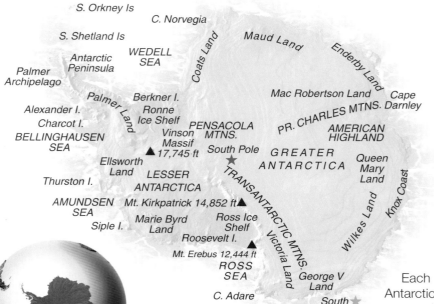

S. Orkney Is · C. Norvegia · S. Shetland Is · WEDELL SEA · Maud Land · Enderby Land · Antarctic Peninsula · Coats Land · Palmer Archipelago · Mac Robertson Land · Cape Darnley · Alexander I. · Palmer Land · Berkner I. · Ronne Ice Shelf · PR. CHARLES MTNS. · AMERICAN HIGHLAND · Charcot I. · PENSACOLA MTNS. · BELLINGHAUSEN SEA · Vinson Massif 17,745 ft · South Pole · GREATER ANTARCTICA · Queen Mary Land · Ellsworth Land · LESSER ANTARCTICA · TRANSANTARCTIC MTNS. · Thurston I. · Knox Coast · AMUNDSEN SEA · Mt. Kirkpatrick 14,852 ft ▲ · Siple I. · Marie Byrd Land · Ross Ice Shelf · Roosevelt I. · Victoria Land · Wilkes Land · Mt. Erebus 12,444 ft ▲ · ROSS SEA · George V Land · C. Adare · South Magnetic Pole

Antarctic melt
Each southern spring, the ice around Antarctica begins to melt, allowing ships to approach the ice shelves around this huge, frozen continent.

FACT BOX

◆ **Arctic Circle**
Area of ocean:
5,506,154 sq miles

◆ **Antarctic Circle**
Area of land:
5,346,154 sq miles

INDEX

Page numbers in *italics* refer to illustrations.

A
Abadan 43
Abbeville 15
Abéché 52
Aberdeen 12, 31
Aberystwyth 13
Abidjan 52
Aboriginal people 56, *56*
Abu Dhabi 43
Abu Simbel *53*
Abuja 52
Abukuma River 4, 49
Acapulco 34
Accra 52
Aconcagua mountain 40
Acropolis 24
Acrtic Circle 6, 60
Adana 42
Addis Ababa 53
Adelaide 56-57
Aden 43
Adriatic sea 24
Aegean 24, *25*
Afghanistan 7, 42, 44-45
Africa 18, 52-3, 54-5
African Americans 30
African people 12, 38
Agra 44, *45*
Agropoli 21
Ahaggar mountains 52
Ahmadabad 44
Ainu people 48
Aix-en-Provence 15
Ajaccio 14
Akita 4, 48
Akron 31
Al Madinah 42
Alabama 31
Alakanuk 32, 60
Alaska 6, 32-33, 60
Alba Iulia 25
Albacete 19
Albania 7, 24-25
Albany 31, 56
Alberta 28, *28*
Albuquerque 30
Alcamo 21
Alcaraz 19
Aldabra Island 55
Alençon 15
Alessandra 20
Alesund 9
Aleutian Islands 32
Aleuts 60
Alexandria 31, 42, 53
Alexandroúpolis 25
Algeria 7, 52, 53
Algerians 14
Algiers 52
Alicante 19
Alice Springs 57
Alkmaar 10, *11*
Allahabad 44

Alma-Ata 26
Almendralejo 18
Almería 19
Alps 4, 14, 16-17, *17*, 20, 49, 56
Alsatians 14, *14*
Altiplano 36-37
Amakusa Island 4, 49
Amarillo 31
Amazon River 5, 36, 38-39, *38*
Amersfoot 10
Amman 42
Amritsar 44
Amsterdam 10
Anadyr' 27, 60
Anchorage 32, 60
Andermatt 16
Andersen, Hans Christian 9
Andes mountains 36-37, *37*, 39, 40
Andorra 7 15, 18-19
Angara 5
Angel Falls 5, 38-39
Anglesey 13
Angola 7, 54-55
Ankara 42
Annapolis 31
Antananarivo 55
Antarctic Circle 6, 60
Antarctica 7, 60, *60*
Antigua 35
Antilles 35
Antwerp 11
Aomori 4, 48
Apeldoorn 10
Appalachian mountains 31, 32
Appenines 20
Arab people 42, 52
Arakan 50
Aral Sea 5
Arawaks 35
Arctic 7, 8, *9*, 26, 28, *29*, 33, 60
Ardennes 10-1
Arendal 9
Argentina 6, 40-41, *40*, *41*
Arizona 30, *31*, 32
Arkansas 31
Arkhangel'sk 26, 60
Arkranes 8
Arles 15
Armagh 13
Armenia 7, 26-27, 30
Arnhem 11, 57
Arnsberg 16
Arran 12
Arras 15
Asahigawa 4, 48
Asian people 12, 38
Astrakhan 26
Asunción 40
Aswân 42, 53, *53*

Asyût 53
Atacama Desert 40
Athens 24-25
Atlanta 31
Atlantic 28
Atlantic Ocean 5, 12, 18, *19*, 28, 30, 35, 38, 53, 54, 60
Atlas Mountains 52
Augusta 31
Aukland 59
Austin 31
Australia 7, 56-57
Austria 7, 16-17
Auxerre 15
Avallon 15
Avezzano 21
Aviero 18
Avignon 15
Ayers Rock 57
Aymara people 36
Azerbaijan 7, 26-27
Aztec 34
Azuaga 18

B
Baden-Baden 16-17
Badwater 33
Baffin Island 5, 29, 60
Bagdad 42
Bahamas 6, 35
Bahia Blanca 41
Bahrain 43
Baja California 34
Bakersfield 30
Balearic Islands 18-19
Bali 50, 51
Balikpapan 51
Balkans *23*, 24-25
Baltic Sea 8, *9*, 17
Baltimore 31
Bandar Abbas 43
Bandung 50
Bangkok 50, *50*
Bangladesh 7, 44, 45, *45*
Bangui 52
Banks Island 60
Barbados 35
Barbezieux 15
Barbuda 35
Barcelona 39
Bareilly 44
Barent's Sea 26 60
baseball *33*
Basel 16
Basingstoke 13
Basques 14
Bass Strait 56, 57
Bassein 50
Bastia 14, 21
Baton Rouge 31
Bavaria *17*
Bay of Bengal 44-45
Bay of Biscay 14, 18
Bayreuth 16
Beaufort Sea 60
Beaumont 31
Beauvais 15
Béchar 52
beer festival *17*
Beijing *46*, 47
Belarus 7, 26
Belgium 7, 10, *10*, 11, 15
Belgrade 25
Belize 6, 34-35
Belmopan 34

Ben Nevis 12
Benelux 10
Benevento 21
Benghazi 52
Benin 7, 52-53
Berber people 52, *52*
Berbera 55
Bergerac 15
Bergisch-Gladbach 16
Bering Sea 60
Bering Strait 27, 32, 60
Berlin 16
Bethel 32
Bhopal 45
Bhutan 7, 44-45
Biarritz 14
Bihac 24
Bilbao 19
Birmingham 13, 31
Bishkek 26
Bismark 31
Biwa Lake 4, 49
Black Sea 24, 42
Blackpool 13
Blenheim 59
Blois 15
Blönduos 8
Boden 8
Bodø 8
Bogotá 36
Bohemia *22*, 23
Boleyn, Anne *13*
Bolivia 6, 36-37, *37*
Bollinäs 9
Bologna *20*
Bombay 45
Bonifacio 14, 21
Bonn 16
Borgarnes 8
Borgholm 9
Borgo 20
Borlänge 9
Borneo 5, 50-51
Bosnia-Herzegovina 7, 24-25
Boston 32
Botany Bay 56
Botosani 25
Botswana 7, 55
Bouake 52
Boulogne 15
Bourg-en-Bresse 15
Bourges 15
Bournemouth 13
Brandenburg 16
Brasília 38-39
Brasov 25
Bratislava 23
Brazil 6, 36-7, 38-39, *38*, *39*
Brazzaville 54
Brest 14
Breton people 14
Bridgwater 13
Brighton 13
Brisbane 56-57
Bristol 13
Britain 38
British Columbia 28
British Isles 7, 12-13
Brittany 14
Bruges *10*, 11
Brunei 7, 50-51
Brunswick 16
Brussels 11, *11*
Bucharest 25
Budapest 22-23, 25

Buddhism 44, 48, *49*, 50, *50*, *51*
Bude 13
Buenaventura 36
Buénos Aires 40-41, *41*
Buffalo 31
Bulawayo 54
Bulgaria 7, 24-25, *24*
Bunbury 56
Bundaberg 57
Burkina Faso 7, 52, 53
Burlington 31
Burma 7, 47, 50, *50*
Burundi 7, 54-55
Bygdeå 9

C
Cabinda 54
Cabot, Sebastian 40
Cádiz 18
Caen 15
Caicos Islands 35
Cairns 57
Cairo 42, 53
Calais 15
Calama 40
Calcutta 45
Calgary 28
Cali 36
California 30, 33
Callao 37
Camagüey 35
Camargue 14
Camarthen 13
Cambodia 7, 50-1
Cambrai 15
Cambridge 13
Cameroon 7, 52-53, 54
Campeche 34
Campo Grande 39
Campos 39
Canada 6, 28-29, *28*, *29*, 30, 32-33, 60, *60*
Canary Islands 52
Canberra *56*
Cancún 34
Cannes 14-15
Canterbury 13
Cape Bathurst 60
Cape Horn 40-41
Cape Lisburne 60
Cape of Good Hope 54
Cape Town 54
Cape Verde Islands 6, 52-3
Cape York Peninsula 57
Capetown 54
Cardiagan 13
Cardiff 13
Caribbean Sea 32, 33, 34-35, *35*, 36, 38
Carlisle 13
Carnarvon 56
Caroline Islands 7, 58
Casablanca 52
Cascade mountains 30, 33
Caspian Sea 5, 26, 42
Catalans 14
Cayenne 39
Cayman Islands 34
Cebu City 51
Cedar Rapids 31
Celtic people 14
Central African Republic 7, 52-53, 54-55

Central America 34-35, *34*, *35*, 36
Central Europe 24
Chad 7, 52-53
Chambéry 15
Changchun 47
Channel Islands 13, 14
Charleston 31
Chartres 15
Chattanooga 31
Cheltenham 13
Cherbourg 14
Chernobyl 26
Cheyenne 31
Chiang Jiang River 5, 46
Chiba 4, 49
Chicago 32
Chile 6, 37, 40-41, *41*
China 5, 7, 44, *44*, 46-47, *46*, *47*, 50
Chinese people 30, 50
Christchurch 59
Christian faith *6*, 42
Chukchi Sea 60
Cincinnati 31
Ciudad Juárez 34
Civray 15
Clyde River 12
Coatzacoalcas 34
Cochabamba 37
coffee *39*
Cognac 15
Cologne 16
Colombia 6, *35*, 36-37
Colombo 45
Colorado 30-31, 32
Columbia 31
Communism 26, 46
Comoros Islands 55
Compiègne 15
Concepción 40-41
Congo 7, 54
Cook Strait 58
Copenhagen 9, *9*
Cordova 32
Cork 13
Cornwall 12
Corpus Christi 31
Corsica 14, 21
Costa del Sol 19
Costa Rica 6, 34-35, *35*
Coventry 13
Crete 25
Croatia 7, 23, 24-25, *25*
Cuba 30, 34-35
Cuzco 37
Cyprus 7, 42-43
Czech Republic 7, 22-23

D
Dakar 52
Dallas 31
Damascus 42
Danes 8
Danube River 16, 17, 22-23, 24
Dar-es-Salaam 54-55
Darling River 56-57
Darmstadt 16
Darwin 57
Davenport 31, 57
Davos 16
Dawson 28, 60
Daytona Beach 31
Death Valley 30, 33
Debrecen 23
Deccan 44-45

61

Delaware 31, 32z
Delft 11
Delhi 44
Democratic Republic of Congo 53, 54-55
Denmark 6-7, 8-9, 28, 60
Denver 31
Derby 13
Detroit 31, 32
Dhaka 45
Dieppe 15
Dijon 15
Dinan 14
Dinant 11
Diyarbakir 42
Djibouti 7, 53, 55
Dôle 15
Dolomite mountains 20
Dominican Republic 6, 35
Donegal 13
Dordogne River 15
Dordrecht 11
Douglas 30
Doula 52
Dover 13, 31
Drakensberg 54
Drama 25
Dubai 43
Dublin 12-13
Dubrovnik 24
Dumfries 12
Dundee 12
Dunedin 59
Dunkerque 15
Durango 30, 34
Durban 54
Durham 13
Düsseldorf 16
Dutch people 10, 11, 35

E
Earth 5
earthquakes 24, 48, 50
East Africa 54-55
East Anglia 12-13
Easter Island 59
Ecuador 6, 36-37
Edinburgh 12
Egypt 7, 42, 52-53, 53
Eindhoven 11
Eire 13
El Paso 30
El Salvador 6, 34-35
Ellesmere 5, 60
England 12-3
Equator 6, 36, 54
Equitorial Guinea 7, 52-53, 54
Erimo Cape 4, 48
Eritrea 6, 7, 42, 53
Essen 16
Estonia 7, 22, 26
Ethiopia 6, 7, 53, 55
Eugene 30
Euphrates River 42
Eureka 30
Europe 8, 10, 12, 14, 17, 18, 24, 26, 33
European Union 6, 10, 12, 14, 17, 18, 20
Exeter 13

F
Fairbanks 32, 60
Faisalabad 44
Falkland Islands 6, 41

Fargo 31
Fiji 7, 58-59
Filippino people 50
Finland 7, 8-9, 60
Fitzroy 56
fjords 8
Flagstaff 30
Flemish people 10
Flinders Range 57
Florence 20
Florida 31, 32
Folkestone 13
Fontainebleau 15
Formentera 19
Formosa 40
Fort Resolution 28
Fort Randall 32
Fort Worth 31
Fort Yukon 32
France 7, 11, 14-15, 19, 30, 32, 38
Frankfurt 16
Franks 14
Fredrikstad 9
Freetown 52
Freiburg 16
Fremantle 56
French Guiana 6, 38-39
Frisians 10
Fukushima 4, 49

G
Gabon 7, 52, 54-55
Galapagos Islands 6
Galatas 25
Gallipoli 21, 42
Gällivare 8
Galveston 31
Galway 13
Gambia 6, 52-53
Ganges River 44
Gävle 9
Geneva 16-7
Genoa 20, 20
Georgia 7, 26-7, 31
Germany 7, 8-9, 11, 15, 16-17, 17, 30, 38
Gerona 19
geysers 58, 59
Ghana 7, 52-53
Ghats 44-45
Ghent 11
Gibralta 18
Gibson Desert 56
Gifu 4, 49
Gijón 18
Gjøvik 9
glaciers 8, 17
Glasgow 12
Gloucester 13
Gobi Desert 46-47
Gold Coast 57
Göteborg 9
Gouda 11, 11
Granada 19
Grand Canyon 30, 32
Granville 14
Great Barrier Reef 56
Great Bear Lake 5, 28
Great Britain 5, 12
Great Dividing Range 56-57
Great Karoo 54
Great Lakes 28, 32
Great Rift Valley 54
Great Salt Lake 30
Great Sandy Desert 56-57

Great Slave Lake 60
Great Victoria Desert 57
Great Wall of China 46
Great Zimbabwe 54
Greece 7, 24-25
Greek Cypriots 42
Greenland 6, 8, 28-29, 29, 60, 60
Greenville 31, 52
Grenada 35
Grenadines 35
Grennock 12
Grenoble 15
Groningen 10
Groznyy 26
Guadalajara 19, 34
Guadeloupe 35
Guadiana River 18
Guatamala 6, 34-35
Guernsey 13, 14
Guinea 6, 52-3
Guinea Bissau 6, 52-53
Gulf of Alaska 60
Gulf of Bothnia 8
Gulf of Carpentaria 56, 57
Gulf of Finland 8
Gulf of Mexico 32, 34
Guyana 6, 38-39

H
Haarlem 10, 11
Hachijo Island 4, 49
Hachinohe 4, 48
Haiti 35
Hakodate 4, 48
Hamamatsu 4, 49
Hamburg 16
Hamilton 29, 59
Hannover 16
Hanoi 50
Harare 54
Hasselt 11
Hastings 13, 59
Havana 34
Havre 30
Hawaii 6, 32-33, 58
Heidelberg 16
Helsinki 8, 9, 60
Henry VIII 13
Highland Games 12
Himalayan mountains 44, 44
Hinduism 44, 45
Hirosaki 4, 48
Hiroshima 4, 49
Hitachi 4, 49
Ho Chi Minh City 50
Hobart 57
Hokkaido 4, 48
Holland 10
Hollywood 33
Homer 32
Honduras 6, 34-35
Hong Kong 7, 46-47
Honolulu 32
Honshu 4, 5, 48-49
Hooper Bay 32
Houston 31
Huang He River 5, 46-47
Hudson Bay 60
Hungary 7, 17, 22-23, 23, 25
Hutchinson 31
Hyderabad 44-45

I
Iberian Peninsula 18-19
Ibiza 19
icebergs 60
Iceland 6, 8, 60
Idaho 30
Ilfracombe 13
Illinois 31
Inca people 36, 36, 37
India 7, 42, 44-45, 45, 50
Indian Ocean 5, 7, 44, 50, 54-5
Indiana 31
Indianapolis 31
Indonesia 7, 50-51, 51, 58
Indus River 44
Ingolstadt 16
Innsbruck 16
Interlaken 16
Inuit people 28, 60, 60
Inverness 12
Iowa 31
Ipswich 13
Iráklion 25
Iran 6, 7, 42-43
Iraq 6, 7, 42-43
Ireland 6, 12-13, 12, 13, 30
Irian Jaya 50-51
Irrawaddy River 50
Ishikari River 4, 48
Islam 42, 44
Islamabad 44
Isle of Man 13
Isles of Scilly 13
Israel 42-3
Istanbul 42
Italy 7, 7, 15, 17, 20-1, 30, 38
Ivory Coast 7, 52-3
Iwaki 4, 49

J
Jacksonville 31
Jaffna 45
Jakarta 50
Jamaica 6, 35
jambalaya 32
Jambi 50
Jamestown 31
Japan 4, 7, 48-9
Java 50, 51
Jefferson City 31
Jefferson, Thomas 7
Jersey 13, 14
Jerusalem 42
Jews 42
Jodhpur 44
Johannesburg 54
John o'Groats 12
Jordan 7, 43
Judaism 42
Jura mountains 14-15, 17
Jutland 8, 9

K
K2 mountain 5, 46
Kabul 44
Kagoshima 4, 49
Kalahari Desert 54
Kalgoorlie-Boulder 56
Kaliningrad 7, 22
Kamaishi 4, 48
Kampala 54
Kanazawa 4, 49

Kansas 31
Karachi 44
Kashmir 44
Kathakali dancers 45
Katmandu 44
Kauai 32
Kawasaki 4, 49
Kayes 52
Kazakhstan 7, 26-27
Kentucky 31
Kenya 7, 53, 54, 55
Khanty-Mansiysk 26
Khartoum 42, 53
Kigali 54
Kilimanjaro 54-55
Killarney 13, 13
Kilmarnock 12
Kimberley 54, 57
kimono 49
Kingston 35
Kingston upon Hull 13
Kinshasa 54
Kirenga 5
Kiribati 7, 59
Kirov 26
Kiruna 8
Kisangani 54
Kitakami River 4, 48-49
Kitakyushu 4, 49
Knoxville 31
Kobe 4, 49
Kochi 4, 49
Kodiak 32
Kofu 4, 49
Komodo 51
Korea 4, 46, 48-49, 30
Koriyama 4, 49
Koshiki Island 4, 49
Kowloon 7
Krakow 23
Kristiansund 9
Kuala Lumpur 50, 51
Kumamoto 4, 49
Kurdish people 6, 42
Kuril Island 4, 48
Kushiro 4, 48
Kuwait 42-43, 42
Kyrgyzstan 7
Kyrgyzstan 26-27
Kyushu 4, 48-49

L
La Louvière 11
La Paz 34, 36-37
La Pérouse Strait 4, 48
La Rochelle 14
Lagos 18, 52
Lahore 44
Lake Baikal 5, 27
Lake Chad 52
Lake Erie 31
Lake Malawi 5
Lake Michigan 5, 32
Lake Nasser 53
Lake Nyasa 55
Lake Superior 5, 31
Lake Tanganyika 5, 54
Lake Titicaca 36-37, 37
Lake Victoria 54-55
Lansing 31
Laos 7, 47, 50-51
Lapland 8, 9
Laramie 31
Las Palmas 52
Las Vegas 30
Latvia 7, 22, 26
Launceston 57

Lawrence River 28
Leaning Tower of Pisa 21
Lebanon 7, 42-43
Leeds 13
Leipzig 16
Lena River 5, 60
Lerwick 12
Lesotho 7, 54-55
Lewis 12
Lexington 31
Lhasa 46
Liberia 6, 52-53
Libya 7, 52-53
Liechtenstein 7, 16-17
Lima 37
Limerick 13
Limpopo River 54
Lincoln 31
Lincoln, Abraham 7
Lisbon 18, 19
Lisieux 15
Lithuania 7, 22, 23, 26
Little Rock 31
Liverpool 13
Livingstone 54
Llanos 38
Locarno 16
Loire River 14, 15
Lomé 52
Lomoges 15
London 13, 13
Londonderry 12
Long Beach 30
Los Angeles 30, 33
Louisiana 31, 32
Lourdes 15
Low Countries 10-11
Lusaka 54
Luxembourg 7, 10-11, 15
Lyon 15

M
Maastricht 11
Macdonnell Ranges 57
Macedonia 7, 24-25
Machu Picchu 36, 37
Mackenzie River 60
Madagascar 5, 7, 55
Madeira 52
Madison 31
Madras 45
Madrid 19
Magyar people 22, 24
Mainz 16
Maitland 57
Malabo 52
Málaga 19
Malawi 7, 54-55
Malaysia 7, 50-51, 51
Maldives 7, 44-45
Mali 7, 52-53
Mallorca 19
Malta 7, 20-21
Managua 34
Manaus 39
Manchester 13
Mandalay 50
Manhattan 32, 33
Manila 51
Manitoba 28, 28
Mannheim 16
Manzanillo 34
Maori people 58
Mar del Plata 41
Marbella 18
Marrakech 52, 52

Marseille 15
Marshall Islands 7, 58-59
Martinique 35
Maryland 31
Masai people *54*
Maseilles 14
Massachusetts 32
Massif Central 14-15
Matsue 4, 49
Matsuyama 4, 49
Mauritania 6, 52-53
Mauritius 7, 55
Maya people 34
Mayenne 15
Mbabane 54
Mecca 42
Medina del Campo 18
Mediterranean Sea 14, 18, 20, 24, 52-53
Mekong River 5, 50
Melanesian people 58
Melbourne 57
Memphis 31
Mende 15
Mendoza 40
Menorca 19
Mexico 6, 30, 32-33, *34*, 34-35
Miami 31
Michigan 31
Micronesia 7, 58-59
Middle East 8, 42, *43*
Middlesbrough 13
Milano 20
Milton Keynes 13
Milwaukee 31
Minneapolis 31
Minnesota 31
Minsk 26
Miskolc 23, 25
Mississippi 5, 31, 32
Missouri 5, 30-31, 32
Mito 4, 49
Miyake Island 4, 49
Miyazaki 4, 49
Moçambique 55
Mogadishu 55
Moldova 7, 26-7
Moluccas 51
Mombasa 54-55
Monaco 7, 14-5
Mongolia 7, 46-47
Monserrat 35
monsoon winds 44, 50
Mont Blanc 15
Montana 30
Montélimar 15
Montenegro 24-25
Montevideo 40-41
Montgomery 31
Montmartre *14*
Montréal 28-9, *29*
Montrose 12
Monument Valley 30, *31*
Monza 20
Morioka 4, 48
Morocco 6, 52-53, *52*
Moscow *6*, 26, *26*, 60
Moselle River 15, 17
Mostar 24
Mount Cook 59
Mount Everest 5, *5*, 44, 46
Mount Fuji 4, 48-9, *48*
Mount McKinley 33
Mount Olympus 25

Mount Pinatubo 51
Mouth Kenya 55
Mozambique 7, 55
Munich 16, *17*
Murmansk 60
Muroran 4, 48
Murray River 56
Muscat 43
Muslim faith *42*, 50
Mutsa Bay 4, 48
Myanamr 7, 47, 50-51, *50*

N
Nagaoka 4, 49
Nagasakai 4, 49
Nagoya 4, 49
Nairobi 55
Namibia 7, 54-55
Nancy 15
Nanda Devi 5
Nanjing 47
Nantes 14
Naples 21
Nashville 31
Nassau 35
Natal 38
Native Americans 28, 30, 34-35, 36, *37*, 38, 40
NATO 33
Nazaré *19*
Nazca 37
Neápolis 25
Nebraska 31
Nelson 59
Nepal *5*, 7, 44-45, *44*
Netherlands 7, 10, *10*, *11*, 30, 38
Nevada 30
Nevis 35
New Brunswick 29
New Caledonia 7, 58
New Delhi 44
New England *30*, 32
New Guinea 5, 50-51
New Hampshire 31
New Jersey 31
New Mexico 30-31
New Orleans 31, 32, *32*
New Plymouth 59
New South Wales *56*, 57, *57*
New York City 31, 32, *33*
New Zealand 7, 58-59, *58, 59*
Newcastle 57
Newcastle upon Tyne 12
Newfoundland 29
Newport 13
Niagara Falls 29, 32
Nicaragua 6, 34-5
Nice 15
Nicosia 42
Niger 7, 52-3
Nigeria 52-3
Niigata 4, 49
Nîmes 15
Nontron 15
Nordhausen 16
Nordvik 60
Norfolk 31
Normandy 14
North Africa 52-53
North Atlantic Ocean 6

North Carolina 31
North Dakota 31
North Island 58-59
North Korea 7, 47
North Pole 60
North Sea 8, 9, 10, 12, 17
Northampton 13
Northern Ireland 12-13
Northern Marianas 33
Northwest Territory 28, 57
Norway 7, 8-9, 60
Norwich 13
Nottingham 13
Nova Scotia 29
Nubian Desert 53
Nullabor Plain 57
Nuremberg 16

O
O-shima 4, 49
Oban 12
Obihiro 4, 48
Odessa 31
Ofenbach 16
Ohio 31
Okavango Delta 54
Okayama 4, 49
Oki Island 4, 49
Oklahoma 31
Olafsjördur 8
Oldenburg 16
Oldham 13
Olekminsk 27
Olympia 30
Oman 7, 43
Omuta 4, 49
Ontario 29, *29*
Orange River 54
Oregan 30, 33
Organization of African Unity 6
Orinoco River 36, 38-39
Orkney Islands 12
Orlando 31
Orléons 15
Osaka 4, 49
Oslo 9
Osnoro 19, 41
Ostend 11
Otaru 4, 48
Ottawa 28-29
Outer Hebrides 12
Oxford 13

P
Pacific 28
Pacific Ocean 5, 28, 30, 33, 34, 36, 50, 58-59, 60
Padua 20
paella *19*
Pakistan 7, 42, 44-45
Palestine 42
Palma 19
Palmero 21
Pampas 41
Panama 6, 34-35, *34, 35*, 36
Papua New Guinea 7, 7, 51, 58-59, *58*
Paraguay 6, 37, 40-41
Paraná River *40*
Paris 14-5
Pasardzhik 25
Patagonia 41

Patna 44
Peace River 28
Pendleton 30
Pennine mountains 13
Pennsylvania 31
Pensacola 31
Penzance 13
Persian Gulf 42, *43*
Perth 12, 56
Peru 6, 36-37, *36, 37*
Perugia 20
Peshawar 44
Peterborough 13
Peterburg 60
Peterhead 12
Philadelphia 31, 32
Philippines 7, 50-51
Phnom Penh 50
Phoenix 30
Pingxiang 47
Pisa 20, *21*
Pizen 23
Plymouth 13
Po River 20
Point Hope 60
Poiters *14*, 15
Poland 7, 22-23, *23*, 30
Polar Lands 60
polders 10
Polynesian people 58, *59*
Pontianak 50
Pontivy 14
population, Earth 5
Port Arthur 31
Port-au-Prince 35
Port Elizabeth 54
Port Harcourt 52
Port Hedland 56
Port of Spain 39
Port Said 42, 53
Port Sudan 42, 53
Portalegre 18
Portland 30
Porto 18
Porto Alegre 39
Porto-Novo 52
Portofino *20*
Portsmouth 13
Portugal 6, 18-19, *19*, 38
Potomac River 30
Potosí 37
Potsdam 16
Prague *22*, 23
Praia 52
prairies 28, *28*, 32
Preston 13
Pretoria 54
Prince Albert 28
Prince Edward Island 29
Prince George 28
Prince Rupert 28, 32
Proserpine 57
Puebla 34
Pueblo 31
Puerto Deseado 41
Puerto Rico 6, 33, 35
Puerto Santa Cruz 41
Puertollano 19
Punjab 44
Pyrenees 14-15, 18-19
P'yongyang 47

Q
Qatar 43
Qena 53
Qingdao 47

Qiqihar 47
Québec 28-29
Quechua people 36
Queen Elizabeth Islands 60
Queensland 57
Queenstown 57
Quetta 44
Quimper 14
Quito 36

R
Ragusa 21
rain forest *34*, 36, 38, *38*, 54
Raipur 45
Raleigh 31
Rameses II *53*
Rangoon 50
Rapid City 31
Rawalpindi 44
Rawson 41
Reading 13
Rebun Island 4, 48
Recife 38
Red Cross 17
Red River 5, 50
Red Sea 52
Redding 30
Redon 14
Reggio 20-21
Reims 15
Renaissance 20
Rendsberg 16
Rennes 14
Republic of Congo 52, 54, 55
Republic of Ireland 12
Republic of South Africa 54
Réunion 7, 55
Reykjavik 8, 60
Rheine 16
Rhine River 16-17
Rhodes 25
Rhône River 14-15
Rhum 12
Richmond 31
Rift valley 53
Riga 22, 26
Rijeka 24
Rimini 20
Rio de Janeiro 38-39, *39*
Rio Grande 30-31, 32, 34
Rishiri Island 4, 48
Rochefort 14
Rochester 31
Rock Springs 30
Rockhampton 57
Rocky Mountains 32
Rodez 15
Roman Catholic Church 20, *23*, 50
Romania 7, 24-25
Rome 20-21
Ronda 18
Rønne 9
Roosevelt, Theodore 7
Røros 9
Rosario 40
Rosenheim 16
Ross Sea 60
Rossano 21
Rostock 16
Rotherham 13
Rotorua 59, *59*

Rotterdam 10-11
Rouen 15
Runta Arenas 41
Russia 7, 8, *23*, 26-27, 30, 33, 60
Russian Federation 6, *6*, 22, 26-27
Rwanda 7, 54-55

S
Saami 8, *9*, 60
Saarbrücken 16
Sacramento 30
Sacré-Coeur *14*
Sado Island 4, 49
Sagami Bay 4, 49
Sahara Dessert 52-3
Sahel 53
Sakai 4, 49
Sakakah 42
Sakata 4, 49
Salem 30
Salinas 30-1
Salisbury 13
Salt Lake City 30
Salta 40
Salvador 38, *38*
Salzburg 16
Samara 26
Samoa 33
Samothrace 25
samurai 48
San Antonio 31
San Bernardino 30
San Diego 30
San Francisco 30, 33
San José 30, 34
San Juan 35
San Marino 7, 20-21
San Salvador 34
San Sebastián 19
Santa Cruz 37
Santa Fe 30
Santa Maria 39
Santiago 41
Santiago de Compostela 18
Santiago de Cuba 35
Santiago del Estero 40
Santo Domingo 35
Santorini *25*
Santos 39
São Tomé 53
São Luis 39
São Paolo 38-39
Sapporo 4, 48
Saragossa 19
Sarajevo 24
Saratov 26, 60
Sarawak 51
Sardinia 20-21
Sasebo 4, 49
Saskatchewan 28, *28*
Saskatoon 28
Saudárkrókur 8
Saudi Arabia 7, 42-43, *43*
Scandinavia 8-9, 28
Scarborough 13
Schffhausen 16
Schweinfurt 16
Schwerin 16
Scotland 12, *12*
Scranton 31
Sea of Japan 48-49
Sea of Okhotsk 60
Seattle 30, 33

Segovia 19
Seine River 14-15
Sendai 4, 49
Senegal 6, 52, 53
Seoul 47
Serbia 24-5
Seville 18, *18*
Seychelles 7, 55, *55*
Sgagerrak 8
Shanghai 47
Shannon River 13
Shantu 47
Sheffield 13
Shelagskiy Mountain 60
s'Hertogenbosch 11
Shetland Islands 12
Shijiazhuang 47
Shikoku 4, 48-9
Shinto faith 48, *49*
Shizuoka 4, 49
Shreveport 31
Shwe Dagon Pagoda *50*
Siam *50*
Siberia 26-27
Sicily 20-21
Siena 20
Sierra Leone 6, 52-53
Sierra Madre 34
Sierra mountains 33
Sierra Nevada 18, 30
Sikh faith 44
Simpson Desert 57
Sinai Peninzula 53
Singapore 7, 50-1
Sioux City 31
Siracusa 21
Siux Falls 31
Skopje 25
Skye 12
slaves 30, 35, 53
Slovakia 7, 22-23
Slovenia 7, 24-25
Smolensk 26
Snowdon 13
Sofia 25
Solingen 16
Solomon Islands 7, 58-59
Somalia 7, 53, 55
Sorong 51
South Africa 7, 54-55
South America 36-37, 38-9
South Atlantic Ocean 6
South Australia 57
South Carolina 31
South China Sea 50-51
South Dakota 31
South Georgia 6, 41
South Island 58-59
South Korea 7, 47
South Orkney Isles 60
South Pacific Ocean 6
South Pole 60
South Shetland Isles 60
Southampton 13
Southeast Asia 50-51
Southend-on-Sea 13
Southern Africa 54-55
Southern Alps 58
Southern Asia 44
Southern Ocean 60
Southwest Asia 42
Soviet Union 22, 26
Spain 7, 18-19, 36, 38
Spanish people 30, 34-35, *37*

Sri Lanka 7, 44-45
St. Basil's Cathedral 6, *26*
St. Brieuc 14
St. Étienne 15
St. Ives 13
St. John's 29
St. Kilda 12
St. Kitts 35
St. Louis 31
St. Lucia 35
St. Malo 14
St. Moritz 16
St. Nazaire 14
St. Petersberg 26, 31
St. Quentin 15
St. Tropez 15
St .Vincent 35
Stanley 41
Statue of Liberty *32*
Stavanger 9
steppes 26
Stockholm 9, *9*, 60
Stoke on Trent 13
Stornoway 12
Strait of Gibraltar 18, 52
Strasbourg 15
Stuttgart 16
Sudan 7, 42, 53, 54
Suez 42, 53
Sumatra 5, 50
sumo wrestlers *49*
Sunderland 13
Sundsvall 9
Sunndalsøra 9
Suo Sea 4, 49
Surabaya 51
Surat 45
Suriname 6, 10, 38-39
Surtsey 8
Swansea 13
Swaziland 7, 54-55
Sweden 7, 8, 9, 60
Swindon 13
Switzerland 7, 15, 16-17, *17*
Sydney 56-57
Sydney Opera House *56*
Syracuse 31
Syria 7, 42-43

T

Tagus River 18
Tahiti 7, 58
Taipei 47
Taiwan 7, 46-7, 51
Taj Mahal *45*
Tajikistan 7, 26-27
Takamatsu 4, 49
Takasaki 4, 49
Takefu 4, 49
Tallahassee 31
Tamale 52
Tampa 31
Tampere 9
Tanega 4, 49
Tangbula *47*
Tangshan 47
Tanzania 7, *54*, 55
Taranto 21
Tashkem 26
Tasmania 56-57
Tbilisi 26
Tegucigalpa 34
Tel Aviv 42
Tennessee 31

Teramo 20
Teresina 39
Teshio River 4, 48
Texarkana 31
Texas 31, 32
Thailand 7, 50-51, *50, 51*
Thames River 13, *13*
The Hague 11
Thessaloníki 25
Thunder Bay 29
Thurso 12
Tiantan *46*
Tibet 7, 46
Tierra del Fuego 40-41
Tigris River 42
Tijuana 34
Timbuktu 52
Timor 51
Tipperary 13
Tobago 35
Tobol'sk 26
Togo 7, 52-3
Tokushima 4, 49
Tokyo 4, 48, 49, *49*
Toledo 19, 31
Toltec 34
Tonga 7, 59
Tornio 8
Toronto 28-29, *29*
Toulouse 15
Tournai 11
Tours 15
Tower of London *13*
Townsville 57
Toyama 4, 49
Toyota 4, 49
Transylvanian Alps 24-25
Tricase 21
Trier 16
Trieste 20
Trikkala 25
Trinidad 31, 35
Trípoli 25, 42, 52
Tropic of Cancer 6
Tropic of Capricorn 6
tropical forests 58
Trujillo 18, 37
Tsugaru Strait 4, 48
Tsushima 4, 49
Tübingen 16
Tucson 30
Tulsa 31
Tunisia 7, 52-53
Turin 20
Turkey 6, 7, 42-43, *42*
Turkmenistan 7, 26-27
Turks Islands 35
Tuvalu 7, 59
Tuzla 24
Twin Falls 30

U

Uberlandia 39
Uchiura Bay 4, 48
Ueda 4, 49
Uelzen 16
Uganda 7, 53, 54-55
Ujung Pandang 51
Ukraine 7, 26-27
Uluru 57
Unalakleet 32
United Arab Emerates 43
United Kingdom 12

United Nations 6
United States Congress *33*
United States of America 6, 7, 28, 30-31, 32-33, 34, 60
Uppsala 9
Uruguay 6, 40-41
Utah 30
Utrecht 11
Utsunomiya 4, 49
Uzbekistan 7, 26-27, *27*

V

Val d'Isère 15
Valencia 19
Valjevo 25
Vancover 28
Vannes 14
Varansi 44
Vatican City 6, 20-21
Venezuela 6, 36, 38-9, *38*
Venica 20, *21*
Veracruz 34
Verona 20
Versailles 15
Vermont *30*, 31
Verona 20
Vesuvius 21
Vichy 15
Victoria 5, 57
Victoria Island 60
Viedma 41
Vienna 15, 17
Vientiane 50
Vieste 21
Vietnam 7, 47, 50-51
Vietnamese people 30, 50
Vikings 8, 14
Villahermosa 34
Villefranches 15
Vilnius 22, *23*
Vilyuy River 60
vineyards *14*
Virgin Islands 33, 35
Virginia 31
Vladivostock 27
volcanoes 33, 34, 48, 50, 54, 58
Volga River 60
Vópnafjördur 8
Vosges *14*

W

Waco 31
Wagga Wagga 57
Wakayama 4, 49
Wakkanai 4, 48
Wales 12
Walloons 10
Walsall 13
Warsaw 23
Washington DC 30-31, 32-33, *33*
Washington, George *7*
Waterford 13
Waterloo 11
Wedell Sea 60
Weisbaden 16
Wellington 59
West Africa 35, 52-53
West Frisian Islands 10
West Palm Beach 31
West Virginia 31
Western Australia 56, *57*
Western Sahara 6, 52-53

Western Samoa 59
Westport 59
Wexford 13
White House 30
Whitehorse 28
Wichita Falls 31
Wiener Neustadt 17
Wigan 13
Wilhelmshaven 16
William the Conqueror *13*
Wilmington 31
Wilson's Promontory 57
Winchester 13
Windsor 31
Winnipeg 28
Winston-Salem 31
Winterthur 16
Wisconsin 31
Wolfsburg 16
Wollongong 57
Wolverhampton 13
World Health Organization 17
World Trade Centre *33*
Worms 16
Wrexham 13
Wroclaw 23
Wuppertal 16
Wyoming 30

X

Xiaguan 47
Xigaze 46
Xinjiang *47*
Xuzhou 47

Y

Yaku 4, 49
Yakutat 32
Yakuts people 60
Yakutsk 27
Yamagata 4, 49
Yamoussoukro 52
Yangon 50, *50*
Yantai 47
Yanomami people *38*
Yaroslavl' 26
Yaroundé 52
Yellowknife 28
Yemen 7, 43
Yenisey River 5, 60
Yeoman of the Guard *13*
Yokohama 4, 49
York 13
Yosemite 5
Yugoslavia 7, 24-25
Yukon Territory 28
Yuma 30

Z

Zaanstad 10
Zagreb 24
Zaïre 5, 7, 55
Zambezi River 54-55
Zambia 7, 54-55
Zamboanga 51
Zanzibar 55
Zaria 52
Zeebrugge *10*, 11
Zermatt 16, *17*
Zhanjiang 47
Zhengzhou 47
Zimbabwe 7, 54-55
Zinder 52
Zurich 17

The publishers wish to thank the artists who have contributed to this book: Julie Banyard; Martin Camm; Mike Foster; Josephine Martin; Terry Riley; Guy Smith; Roger Smith; Michael White/Temple Rogers.

The publishers would like to thank the following for supplying photographs for the Atlas

Page 5 (T/R) MKP; 5 (B) PhotoDisc; 6-7, 9, 10-11 all MKP; 12 (C/R) & (B/L) Spectrum Colour Library; 14 (T/R) MKP; (B/L) & (B) The Stock Market; 15 (B) MKP; 17 (C/R) & B/R) The Stock Market; (B) MKP; 18 (B) MKP; (T/R) & (B/R) The Stock Market; 20-21, 24-25 all MKP; 26 (T/C) MKP; (B/C) The Stock Market; 28 (B/C) The Stock Market; 29 (T/R) The Stock Market; 30 both MKP; 32-33 (C) MKP; 33 (C) The Stock Market; 33 (B/R); MKP; 34 (T/L) MKP; 34 (B) The Stock Market; 35 (C) MKP; 37 (T/L) The Stock Market; (B/C) PhotoDisc; 38 (B/L) MKP; 39 (T/R) PhotoDisc; (C) & (B/R) The Stock Market; 40-41 all Sue Cunningham Photographic; 42-43 all MKP; 44 (T/L) MKP; 45 (C/R) The Stock Market; (B) MKP; 46 (T/R) The Stock Market; (B) & (B/C) MKP; 47 (C/R) MKP; 48 (T/R) & (C) MKP; 49 (C/R) MKP; (B/C) The Stock Market; 50-51 all MKP; 52-53 all MKP; 54-55 all The Stock Market; 56 (T/R) & (B/L) MKP; (B/C) The Stock Market; 58-59, 60-61 all MKP